How to Get Hired

How to Get Hired

Job Market Secrets Every Grad Needs to Know

Jill DeSena-Shook

Wisdom Moon Publishing
2016

HOW TO GET HIRED

JOB MARKET SECRETS EVERY GRAD NEEDS TO KNOW

Published by Wisdom Moon Publishing LLC
San Diego, CA, USA

www.WisdomMoonPublishing.com

ISBN 978-1-938459-46-7 (softcover, alk. paper)
ISBN 978-1-938459-48-1 (eBook)
LCCN 2016942769

How to Get Hired

Job Market Secrets Every Grad Needs to Know

"We are shut up in schools and college recitation rooms for ten or fifteen years, and come out at last with a bellyful of words and do not know a thing."

-Ralph Waldo Emerson (1803-82), U.S. essayist and poet

How to Get Hired

How I Started My Dream Job And Then Began My Real Job

One day, in my senior year at college, my Communications professor told me to get on the bus that was loading up students. When I asked where it is going, he said, "ABC studios. They are hiring their interns today. Come on! Come with us!" I did.

Sitting in the waiting area for the programs *20/20* and *Live! With Regis & Kathy Lee* (Kathy came before Kelly for those of you who were in grade school at the time). I noticed that I was not...pretty, like the other 50 plus young women waiting on line to meet with the producers of these shows. They all had nicer features and thinner legs than me. I can remember thinking to myself, "You are not TV material, Jill; you'd better ask for a back office job."

When it was my turn to sit with a producer for an interview I said: "I really don't want to intern at *Live,* I would rather do *20/20*, something with research." I went on to explain myself and why I was there. I remember that I had no clue as to what this guy interviewing me was thinking. I did not know if he liked me or not. I couldn't read him at all. And you know what? That is still the same today. Usually you won't be able to read the people interviewing you.

At this point in my life, my only work experience was as a waitress, which I had done for three years in order to pay for college. I was good at it. Under pressure, I could quickly and accurately deliver food and drinks to lots of people. This was all I had to fall back on. I recall saying something like, "After ten tables a night for three years, I can be the best intern in the world." I guess it worked because I was hired as an intern for the show *Live! With Regis & Kathy Lee.* From 100+ applicants that day, I was one of only ten girls that made the cut. Good thing I got on the bus, huh?

Soon after starting at *Live!* the guy who chose me for the internship told me why. One, I didn't care about being *discovered* and meeting celebrities, like those girls with the nice legs, and two, I wanted to "serve people." That is exactly what the internship required...a waiter without tips. He knew because he had been an intern just five years earlier. From the beginning, my expectation of the job was correct. And because I was able to express that in the interview, the producer knew that I would not be offended when someone asked for coffee. Or a lightly toasted dry cinnamon bagel, scrambled egg whites, and a venti, extra hot, decaf, sugar free, hazelnut, skim latte—as Bette Midler did.

When the internship was over and I received my degree, I had a hard time searching for a job. Eventually, I was hired by *ABC Studios* as a Production Assistant. My salary was $18,000 a year. Work hours were: 7 am to 7 pm, Monday to Friday. That's right: that is TV. The big salaries go to the big names, not to the little people behind the scenes. This was the job that I had paid my way through school (as a broadcasting and journalism major) to get. I was making less than minimum wage just to get my foot in the door. And those student loan bills ate up most of my salary.

After almost a year at *Live!* I was ready to move on. I no longer wanted to work in television. Celebrities weren't interesting anymore: you never really "meet" a celeb: you just "see" them. Big deal, they look like people, only thinner with better skin. I wanted to see what else was out there. I was tired of making very little money for working such long hours. When I asked Executive Producer Michael Gilman for a raise, I recall him reminding me how lucky I was to have a job there.

"Do you know how many people in this country wish they had your job?" At the time, I felt like saying "Do you know how it feels to do slave labor in a free country like America?" And he probably would have answered yes. Michael Gilman was an intern at *Live!* He stuck it out for years. Now he is the Executive Producer of one of the most successful morning shows in the history of television. Back then I never thought I would say this but I am forever grateful to Michael Gilman for giving me a chance. He let me work there. He gave me something...it is called *opportunity*. My small paycheck and long hours spent at the job were not what I had envisioned for myself, but at least I was working. Plus, I was single and had no one to care for but myself. I got by. I worked my heart out. I learned a lot about the work ethic at that television show.

When I wanted to find a new job, I went to my older sister who always seemed to know what to do. She went to school in New York City and lived there for years. She got me in contact with her friend Angela, who was a "temp." Angela suggested that I go to her "agency." I was told that an employment agency on Madison Avenue had recruiters who "found people jobs"—for free! Having never heard of an employment agency, I went in to meet with a recruiter. After interviewing for a few hours, with various people, the agency itself actually hired me to work for them. I was now an Account Manager for a mid-size recruiting agency in New York City. Soon I was recruiting employees for temporary and permanent job openings and interviewing anywhere from five to ten candidates a day.

Opportunity Knocks!

At no other time in recent history will more people be competing for the same jobs than now. When companies decide to re-hire as we crawl out of the recent mess of a recession, they are hiring more entry-level workers. It is already starting to happen. Why? Entry-level workers cost less money, most have a degree, and they are highly experienced already with emerging technology and software. You grew up with computers and are the future of the American work force. Those of you entering the workforce for the first time have an incredible opportunity. Now, if you could just write a good resume, present yourself well, and say the right things on an interview, you'll be golden. Unfortunately that is not always as easy as it sounds and many of you need help. You need to be aware of things you are not aware of when dealing with a job search. You need to be *warned* about what TO DO and what NOT TO DO concerning everything from resumes to job offers. If an employer does open your resume attachment, I want to make sure they call you and not delete it. If someone does interview you, I want to make sure they give you an offer and do not discount you.

Finally, Someone Who Can Help You

During the past twelve years I have placed thousands of temporary and full-time people into law firms, banks, accounting firms, fashion houses, television studios, and hotels. As a recruiter, my talent is in my choice. The people I choose to send out for an interview will ultimately make or break my career, so I must prepare them well. I truly care about the job seekers who need guidance. Those of you looking for jobs are not a product to be sold. Taking the time to teach people about resumes and interviewing is how I have grown my business and become a successful recruiter in New York City.

How to Get Hired

Being a professional recruiter for over a decade has given me an insight that very few are privy to. Five days a week I discuss resumes, interview techniques, and job offer negotiation with applicants **and** employers. I know the type of person a company will hire because I was trained the hard way.

On more than one occasion, I have had my ears turn bright red and felt like I was going to be sick because a client (whom I worked so hard to get) told me that my applicant had made a jackass of him- or herself. Ultimately they made a jackass out of me. The client wanted to know why I wasted their time and sent that person in for an interview. Having that feeling in the pit of your stomach makes you prepare applicants better and avoid making that mistake again. Talk about pressure. Over the years I have done everything possible to coach applicants for the hiring process. Not only so that they will get the job, but also so that they will not embarrass me. I recognize that, as a recruiter, I am accountable. Through trial and error I have learned how to train your ordinary job seeker into the viable candidate who gets the job offer.

The people I enjoy working with the most are recent college graduates or anyone who is new to the job market. They are unemployed and often in debt. They are a blank canvas. They are the ones with whom I spend the most time explaining what is in these pages.

Getting them their first job offer is gratifying. I want *you* to understand why certain people do not get hired and why some, even after many failed interviews, finally get a great job. And for those of you who do not have recruiting firms in your area: this is important information for you especially. It will give you the edge you need and tip you off to the mistakes others have made that cost them the offer.

Are You in the Dark? – Let's Turn On the Light

First off, your resumes are not helping your cause. Where did you learn to write it? Perhaps a "How To" guide with generated examples? Maybe you got help writing your resume from an Internet site or from your friends. Did you have a job description to consider when you starting constructing your resume? It is the job description (and not your OBJECTIVE) that is the first step in writing a resume. With examples of *real* resumes in chapter three you will see how even the subtlest changes will get you an interview. My resume formula *will* get you an interview. It is *proven*. This simple formula helped me advance from an Account Manager to Vice-President in just four years. It is the secret of my success.

Now that I have all but promised you an interview, I'm not about to let you blow it. We are going to talk *point-blank* about your appearance—what to wear and how to speak—as it will demonstrate many things to your interviewer.

The "ABCs" chapter will explain what is expected of your **A**ttitude, **B**ehavior, and **C**haracter. I don't want you to "sell yourselves" on any interview—*you are not for sale*. I want you to *show yourself*. By applying your ABCs to the interview process, you will shine.

When it comes to interviewing, some of my recently hired graduates have shared their own stories. Truth is, they were on the interviews, not me and their perspective is crucial. Read what worked for them and what they said or did that made things go terribly wrong.

Jill DeSena-Shook

This book embodies my experience as a recruiter. Everything that you are about to read here has been told to hundreds of my applicants. The best days are when I see the light bulb go on - I love that look on their face. They smile, they nod their head, they sit up straight, and they are in someway stronger.

Now they are excited and confident because they suddenly "get it." It is only a matter of time until they get hired. *Will* you *get it?*

Let's begin...

Testimonials

"After months of being unable to find a job, I was referred to Jill DeSena by a friend. At first I didn't understand what Jill would be able to do for me that I wasn't capable of doing myself. What I soon realized was that Jill could do a lot for me based on my initial meeting with her.

"Finding a job today is difficult, especially with the economy the way it is. It's difficult to do it alone. Jill was an invaluable tool for me because her knowledge of the employment field and the firm I interviewed with gave me an edge over the candidates who came in on their own.

"Her tips on what to wear, how to restructure my resume, and what to be prepared for on the interview gave me the confidence on my interview that I needed to impress the employer. With six other people applying for the same job, all of whom were as qualified and experienced as I was, some even more, I was able to get the job because I stood out as being prepared, and employers know that if you're prepared on an interview, you'll be prepared on the job."

-Bill H.

"Jill is a recruiter of the highest order. She succeeds continually in matching the skills of the job-seeker to the needs of the client with insight and precision. Jill has placed me in the most challenging atmosphere, providing satisfaction beyond expectations and an opportunity for me to shine. She accomplishes her objectives with integrity, sensitivity, grace, and irresistible charm. Jill brings paramount professionalism and forthright character to every situation. I would heartily recommend her."

-Diane B., Esq.

"Jill DeSena: she's more than a recruiter. She's your lawyer, your friend, and someone that makes you feel good when you feel that there is no hope in getting a position; especially during these times. She got me a job when ALL other agencies said it was virtually impossible to get one. She fought for me and sold me better than anyone I've ever dealt with. AND SHE EVEN RETURNED CALLS!!!"

-Edward C.

"Jill is a recruiter. But she is no one's idea of 'typical,' nor does the word 'average' apply. Though she may work primarily behind the scenes, Jill makes miracles happen for real people. Savvy, pragmatic, supportive, enthusiastic and charming. THESE are the genuine qualities she brings to any hiring situation."

-Gloria P.

"Jill has the best clients in the city. They are doing the most high profile work in the industry and they absolutely demand that their employees meet the high standards of professionalism that success in their industry requires. They also maintain a unique corporate culture that even the smartest college graduate would take years to fully comprehend.

"Jill has many years of experience preparing her candidates to land jobs in these highly coveted positions. She knows the market better than anyone else and she has successfully placed hundreds of candidates in these positions. My own experience confirms that anyone seeking one of these jobs can create demand among employers by following her advice."

-Ian M.

"Jill sent me on interviews feeling confident, comfortable and fully prepared to meet with prospective employers. I always felt that she was looking out for my best interests and not just sending me out on anything they had, like other agents I worked with. She helped me truly believe that the 'right' spot would come along and not to take a position be-

cause I was anxious. She was right. I am so grateful I was referred to Jill. She is a consummate professional and a pleasure to work with."
-Renee D.

"Jill was a huge help in placing me at one of the top financial law firms in New York City. Before I came to her, I had learned a lot from trial and error. When I enlisted her help in my job search, I realized that if I had started out with her, I would have been in far better shape early on. She knows exactly what employers are looking for, and she's excellent at matching applicants with clients so that both parties are happy. If there's any advice I could give—fifteen months after she placed me and with the job market more competitive than ever—it'd be to heed her advice."
-Jason R.

"Many recruiters will tell you anything to try to 'sell' you on a position (just so they can get their fee). Not so with Jill. Jill is a highly respected recruiter who has the wisdom to want both her clients and the firms she works with to be happy. She takes the time to learn about the needs and goals of both and takes great care to create happy and productive relationships. She will tell you the 'real deal'! Job shopping can be nerve wracking, but working with someone like Jill, being prepared with your resume, learning the 'tools' of interviewing, and remembering to breathe and have confidence in being you...you position yourself to come out winning!"
-Claudia D.

"In my experience with Jill, she was very encouraging and supportive. Interviewing is hard, now imagine doing it alone, blindfolded. Recruiters like her have an inside look into the company and are able to guide you and make you feel comfortable with the interview process. Jill took the time to get to know me and understood my resume (my abilities) and got me a job that suits my schedule need and my personality. She was great through this whole process. I would not have my job without her."
-Caroline M.

"Jill is incredibly diagnostic about finding an appropriate fit for the people she represents. She has a pragmatic approach, but one that does not sacrifice compassion for you as an individual or for your interests and strengths, be they what they may. She is honest, approachable, and 100% vested in finding the best fit for you. Though I cannot speak from personal experience, it is my understanding that this is not always the case with other placement agencies in the city: often the humanity and personal rapport that constitute Jill's creed are lost somewhere in the shuffle. She understands what it means to be young and unsure of where to tread; she is a wonderful mentor and an unwavering advocate. I cannot emphasize enough how encouraging it is knowing you have someone on your side. And Jill was always on my side."
-Laurel H.

How to Get Hired

Post Graduation Journal: WEEK 1

Finally! I have my degree. I finished college and an internship. That $100,000 piece of paper, commonly known as a diploma, is being framed at the frame store this very minute. My parents are proud of me. I feel pretty good. I will feel even better once someone starts paying me. I mean, all the work I did for four years; I better make a hefty paycheck. But it is not all about the money. Of course it should pay well, but it also has to be something that I want to do: something exciting. Something that shows off my talents, you know? I have a lot to offer, so I want a job where I can make a difference in the world.

I have a resume and I gotta tell ya, it's damn good. I have some friends who took the resume business lightly, writing something up in one short afternoon (stopping for some refreshment breaks along the way). They think they have an impressive document for potential companies to be impressed by.

For me, I knew that this was serious business and so I worked on it in steps and stages, over a full week, reviewing, changing some phrases, and polishing the text. I had my good friends Kim and Debbie (who both are English majors) to work with, and we created the perfect summary of my life's achievements thus far.

I just got a new suit on sale at the department store. It is a real professional type suit. It is perfect for interviewing and at 50% off. Could I get any luckier? The legs are a bit long, so I bought a pair of high heels. Those shoes kill my feet but are high enough so that I don't have to hem the pants. I spent a little too much on the shoes but soon enough I will be bringing home the bacon. I have one of those business-type briefcases. It is a very cool green leather bag from the Kate Spade Outlet. My sister bought it for me as a graduation present. What else do I need? Nada! I am so ready to get out there and start earning and making my mark in the world.

Now who will interview me? I know I will be an asset for any company. I was, by the way, an intern at a pretty big company. I wonder how much money I can make? I hear people earn good starting salaries with a college degree and I graduated from a good school. I bet if I call the career counselor's office, they can set me up with a bunch of interviews. Maybe my professors have a few contacts and I know my parents do. I should have a job in like a month tops. Then after a few months at work, I can take a Spring Break vacation with my friends and get paid while I am on the beach. Ah, I love being out of school. The good life I worked so hard for awaits me.

Post Graduation Journal: WEEK 12

What the hell is up with that Career Counselor's office? They never got back to me with even one job interview. I did everything they told me to. I have sent a resume to every company that I could possibly see myself working for, and not one call? My suit is getting dust on the shoulders. What is wrong with these people? It must be the economy.

My parents are getting on my nerves too. All damn day, it is either "So how's the job hunt going?" or "Why don't you do something around town to pay your bills in the mean time" or "Did you call my friend Doug over at Sun Bank? He said there might be something opening up." Don't they understand what I am going through right now? Obviously they don't. How could they? I mean they have a job: someone is paying them every Friday! They think it's so easy. I didn't spend four years working my ass off to answer phones for Doug at friggin' Sun Bank! I have a degree from a good school.

Post Graduation Journal: WEEK 20

Okay, is this some kind of cruel joke? Does not *one company* in this God forsaken state need a qualified college graduate? ANY COMPANY? Why doesn't *anyone* respond to my resume? At this point, I don't even know how many times I've sent it out, or to which companies; I've lost track. I check my email every hour and not one response. Doug from Sun bank didn't even call me back after I went *all* the way over there to meet the guy. This might take longer that I expected. I am out of money and my student loan bills have already starting coming in the mail. Maybe I should go back to school. Things were much easier when I was in college. No one is helping me! All they say is *get a job*. HOW? I can't even get an interview! No one will even see me. My parents and everyone else thinks it's so easy. They do not understand how hard I am trying. My life right now...in plain English...sucks.

Jill asks, Now What?

I remember how I felt after graduation: it was a rough time. But everyone gets through it and so will you. That's right...so will YOU.

After graduation, I did not know any of the secrets written in these pages. I had the degree but knew nothing about how to get a job that required one. I didn't even know what a *recruiter* was. No one tells you *how* to get a job; they just keep telling you to get one and don't offer up any solid leads that will help you. This may be the first time in your life you cannot find help when you really need it.

But you must have some idea of how you will begin. What is your plan? The career services center at your college? At a certain point, it is not enough. A college counselor's job is never in jeopardy when you don't get hired. Career services try to be helpful. Unfortunately however, many do not know what to do when a student can't get hired. Most of these counselors do not speak to *employers* intimately enough to know exactly what to do to get hired. Much more goes into job-hunting than your resume and a blue or black suit.

If you begin this quest on-line you are simply entering into a black hole. Career Builder.com, CraigsList.com, Monster.com, Hot Jobs, the list goes on and on. These search engines are becoming over-crowded with resumes. There are millions of resumes on these job sites. How do you make yours stand out and get an employer to call you? I have the answers for you.

Truth is, no one really *knows* for sure how to go about getting hired, except recruiters. Recruiters spend their careers getting people jobs. If they don't get someone a job, they don't get paid. So if you make a living as a recruiter chances are you know what to do. I am a recruiter. It is my job to know how to get someone hired.

Chapter One

HELP YOURSELF - RESEARCH YOUR INTERESTS

"No one cares more about you than you."
-Peter J. LaPlaca, Ph.D. (Author, Editor, Marketing Professor)

Do you know why you feel like no one is helping you? It's because no one is helping you. Ultimately, you have to get the job on your own. Your college career counselors and professors have only so much time for each senior. Your parents can only do so much and their time taking care of you is finished. If it is not finished in your opinion, let me tell you something: *they* would like it to be. Even though some parents don't admit it to their kids, or even themselves, they want you to stand on your own two feet now. Take the ball and run with it, the sooner the better.

The way you prepare for this time period in your life is extremely important. Yes—you read that correctly—you must *prepare* for the job search phase of your life BEFORE you actually create and send out your resume and cover letters. Getting a diploma and buying a suit do not prepare you for a job interview. You must give attention and focus to research prior to becoming employed.

The Time is Now
You will begin with: Research & Documentation, Networking, and Authority. Don't waste time and delay your preparation. Again, the sooner you begin to apply these concepts in your life, the faster you will get a job. Especially when you do not have a recruiter.

Research: Expand Your Knowledge
In the same way you began looking at colleges in your sophomore and junior years of high school, you should start collecting information on industries of interest while you are still in college. Law, finance, health care, sales, government, fashion, education—the possibilities are endless.

"Interest is the Mother of Attention - Attention is the Mother of Memory."
This research begins the marketing and business development of *you*. In order to recall information and competently discuss an industry during a conversation (like an interview) you must learn something about it first. If you lack experience in a certain field you must *at least* have knowledge of it. Finding out *why* an industry moved in a certain direction will increase your knowledge on *every* company in the field.

> *People respect research and knowledge on their company*
> *but more importantly on their industry.*

This will never replace experience, but it can create a connection to that line of work. It also *proves* that you are aware of and can study *strategies* in business. On an interview, you will be able to speak intelligently about the industry's history and development and you will *prove* your curiosity to learn more. It will show a potential employer that you *want to be there.*

Documentation - Tailor It All To ...YOU

That's right ... this is about *your personal interests* and the industry you hope to work in. Don't feel like this is work for a report. YOU are the student and the teacher. You are deciding what is interesting and what is a total bore. You make all the decisions. And don't you dare let mom or dad or Uncle Fred make those decisions for you. They do not care more about you than you. Tell them I said so.

As you continue your research, you will find yourself drawn to specific companies and organizations. Take notes and build files on the different industries and professions that interest you.

* * *

You should prepare and retain files, organized by both INDUSTRIES and COMPANIES.

Now, talk about an advantage that prior generations did not have! They don't call it the "information-highway" for nothing. You lucky dogs! I wish, I wish, I wish I had the Internet when I was younger. You can research an industry so completely and so quickly. Newspaper articles and professional journals at your fingertips will provide you with the history, trends, emerging software, hires, fires, capital gains and losses, new technology, the big players involved and who works with them and for them. You can get annual reports. The product literature may also be available if that company mass produces products. Research it all! Everything you can Google, Google! Then print it out and keep it in the correct folder for your future reference.

Networking

Organizations and Associations and their respective Board Members can also be found quickly on line. Search for "associations" *in your geographical area* that are specific to certain industries of interest. The Board of Directors at these associations will be important contacts. Find out who they are and where they work. These associations are in big cities and small towns everywhere. Research the *Association of Marketing Professionals* nearest you if you are interested in that industry. Contact the *Association of Legal Administrators* if you want to be a paralegal. Then call up and make a connection. The right way is to be humble and simply look to *learn about that industry*. **The wrong way is to ask for a job**. Don't mention getting a job. If you do, you blew it. Ask for a tour. Ask to speak to someone in the association regarding information on the industry. Ask to interview *them* on business development in their industry. LISTEN AND LEARN from them and gather notes and information for your files.

If you are granted a tour or a visit (and it goes well), ask about volunteering or interning in their office. Okay, now some of you just read that and are thinking, "Yeah right, I'm not doing that"...but others are going to do it and just might get a job that you lazy people missed. Perhaps you have to be desperate in order to stop saying "Yeah right, I'm not doing that." I know a lot of young people who say "Yeah right, I'm not doing that." And guess what? They are right. A year out of college and they are still *not doing* ANYTHING.

Believe it or not, most of the professionals in these organizations want to help you if you are willing to learn and extend yourself. Honestly, they do. They love their industry or they wouldn't be part of the association in the first place. When they see an eager person who is just reaching out asking to learn (and being sincere about it) they will try to, not just teach, but help. They want to give guidance and share their knowledge.

Don't be shy. You can't afford to be.
If they do grant you a tour or a meeting, dress to impress when you arrive and *be in the moment*. Be attentive and follow all that they say with good eye-contact and appreciation. Request business cards from everyone and anyone you meet, even secretaries. Trust me, the secretaries are the quiet force that runs an office. If they want their boss to look at something, or sign a letter, or take a call, they make it happen. With time you can gather many contacts in your fields of interest.

"I've gotten better at not making people feel uncomfortable with my shyness."
Clea DuVall, actress

Being shy is all about YOU. Remember that. It is not about anyone else but you. You are a normal person, just like everyone else. There is never any reason to be shy. If you are, you are simply forcing others to feel uncomfortable around you. When you have the opportunity to meet and talk to others and network, try not to act that way. The way you make others feel is the only thing they take away when the meeting is over. *They remember you by how you made them feel.*

After meeting contacts, write a handwritten thank-you note in your best handwriting and on a plain, professional type of note card. Even if someone just spent time with you on the phone talking about business and giving you information on an industry or company, send them a thank you. It *proves* you appreciate whatever time they gave you.

Keep That Card!
Business cards are important for your files. Collect business cards while looking polished, being eager and interested. On the back of the card, write down the date and circumstances of your meeting or introduction. These cards may be helpful in the future.

If you do that, you may never have to ASK for a job at all: someone may eventually just offer you one. And even if they don't, you can at least have a contact in the business or at that company if you apply for a job. Also those contacts can tell you about jobs in their industry as well.

Word of Mouth: The Best Networking Tool Around

You can't beat it. It will never go out of style. It is still the fastest, most convenient, and most definite way to gain (or lose) trust in something or someone. One person telling another about someone or something can be the most valid form of reference. It is almost always backed up with experience. The person giving the suggestion had an experience and so now they KNOW. They pass the word on.

Utilize every last contact that you have when networking. Again, *don't ask for a job*, even with these contacts. Just be patient and gather knowledge and prove that you are *eager and appreciative.*

"I ate at the best *restaurant last night! Prices are good and the food is outstanding."*

This is how a restaurant can get put on the map and it is how networking people can get a interview.

"If you have an opening, you really should meet Dylan Wright. He is just the nicest guy. He came in here a few months ago and was just an all-around polite, intelligent, young man. Give him a call. He'd be perfect for that entry level spot."

If a respected board member of an association says that to a colleague, well then that is that. Dylan IS someone they have to meet. If Dylan just follows what is written in the rest of this book, he is going to get hired so fast it will make his head spin.

U.S. Societies & Associations

A comprehensive listing of some 23,000 national and international organizations are in the directory called The Encyclopedia of Associations.

Authority and Being Present in Your Job Search

If you DO work with a recruiter and do not document information and network, you are foolish. If you DO NOT work with a recruiter and you do not document information and network you are in jeopardy of wasting time (months...perhaps years) searching for a job. You may even end up accepting a job you don't want in an industry you don't want. That is not a positive way to begin a career or rest of your life.

So be in control. You've always wanted control - here it is! Smile and grab on to it. My point is: whether you have a recruiter working with you or not, you must BE YOUR OWN RECRUITER. Network and find information about companies and industries at any organization or association or alumni luncheon or college program or town hall meeting. Get out there and show yourself to people working in your industries of interest. They won't bite, I promise.

Your recruiter bites. They don't.

How to Get Hired

Internships

Internships are your opportunity to gain important knowledge and experience in various professions. Your college's career counselors will be very helpful in this endeavor. They not only know about the various alumni associations within your fields of interest, but they have the contacts for those coveted internships.

Internships are usually unpaid, so finding someone to accept a free employee should not be that hard. Start with your college's career services center, but do not limit yourself. ANYONE you know who may work in a desired field, should be a resource. After friends and family a wise thing to do is get a list of your school's alumni on line.

Reach out to all these contacts. Ask them who you can speak to about interns at their company and if they would give you a good reference if need be.

Internships let you go for a test drive. You may gain helpful contacts and experience that will help you after graduation; or you may simply find that a seemingly interesting profession is not your cup of tea. Either way, utilizing internships for all they have to offer will aid you in your research. Also use the internet: www.internships.com is a terrific website to begin on. You can find internships in your area also by simply using the Internet. If your career counselor cannot set you up, then set yourself up. But DO get an internship under your belt. It is important, especially if you did not work at all while you attended college. If you get college credit for it, that's great. If not, get off your butt and do it anyway.

The Pay Off

From your research you will narrow down where you'd like to apply for a job. What is a certain company doing that is superior and made you want to apply for a job with them rather than the competition? Now you have something to put in a cover letter that is attractive to that employer.

> *Internships are GIFTS. Most times they lead to employment in one way or another.*

Check websites of companies that are of interest and see if they are hiring. If nothing is on their web site about openings, call and check with their Human Resources Department. If the company is hiring, HR will let you know—I promise. If they say "not at this time," then ask where they will post job openings when they are looking to hire. Most times they will say, "on our website." So keep checking and move on to other companies and other industries. You live in a busy country with opportunity everywhere...Lucky you!

Remember: You may have to take the long road to get the position at company you want to work with. The best thing to do is focus on either getting hired at your desired company in a lesser position or in that industry with a smaller company.

For example:

1. Get a job in the mailroom or as a receptionist or an administrative assistant (wherever they will hire an entry-level worker) and quietly work

your way up. I say *quietly* because if you interview for one job but tell them you eventually want a different job, you will NOT GET THE JOB.

2. Get a job at a smaller company in the same industry and then keep trying to get an interview at the larger company. Gain experience while you wait with a plan in mind. Your resume will look better to the larger company now because you have experience in the same industry.

Right now, you first stgeop is to gain experience. You must start somewhere. So get over yourself and realize that your first paying job is a gift. That's right... someone is *giving* you a chance, PLUS they are paying you. It is a real pain in the ass to train someone, even if they had a 4.0 in college. If someone is willing to train you in any area of interest, then *get on the bus.*

What Do You Want to Be When You Grow Up?

One thing I learned early on and still notice everyday about people and their jobs is this: Most people don't know what they want to be when they grow up, even grown-ups. Many workers get their first job in an industry that they originally found appealing after getting their degree. Then after a few years of working in that field, they are disheartened and feel unfulfilled. A lot of these people feel stuck in that line of work because it is their only experience. Some spend years hating what they do. Before you start this job-hunting process you must realize that *you are never trapped in any career*. If you apply yourself and are willing to work at it, you can always change fields. Sometimes people get into a career with no knowledge of an industry and love it. Whatever you do just make sure you love your industry. In the beginning you may not love your job but do you love the industry? I honestly did not even know what a recruiter was the day before I was hired to be one. But you know what? Twelve years later, I love it. My job is like a hobby to me.

Chapter Two

GETTING DISCOVERED

How Do I Get a Chance with No Experience?
Please, keep in mind your biggest strengths: youth, low salary expectation and computer proficiency.

Youth
Current employees don't feel like making copies or going to the post office every day or cleaning up the conference room or ordering lunch or running out to *Staples.* They are tired of doing that. You're not! At least you shouldn't be. You should be happy to pitch in doing WHATEVER—WHEREVER—WHENEVER.

Money
Most adults need to make $30,000 to $50,000 a year just to cover the mortgage. You probably don't have a mortgage so you can take the job for less.

Computers
Be creative and use your strengths. We all didn't grow up with computers...but you did! Let them know you have extensive experience using creative software. You possess a thought process that involves the utilization of computer software more often and in more ways. This premise will tie *you* and *the company* together with one word...FUTURE.

THE PROCESS OF USING A RECRUITER

Ok, you have sent out more than a hundred resumes on-line, complete with a well-crafted cover letter and yet, not one response. Why no calls for an interview? Your resume is one of hundreds, if not thousands being submitted for the same job. Most likely your resume doesn't match the job description (more on that later). But just as important, no one is calling on your behalf.

"You can't get a job without first getting an interview, and I learned the hard (and slow!) way that getting an interview is hard. One thing that makes this first step exponentially easier is having a connection, whether it be your sorority sister's step-uncle or a recruiter. I didn't have any connections in the field I wanted to enter. Despite graduating with honors from a highly ranked liberal arts school, I did not receive any responses from the 50+ positions I applied to "cold" online. To be honest, had I received an offer to interview for any of these positions, I probably would have botched it. It was not until after I sat down with Jill that I was properly prepared to show myself in the best light. No matter how bright and talented you are, or how well your college has prepared you for the real world, in today's market you need to capitalize on any advantage you can. Jill was my advantage."
-Erin C.

"Help me help you"
There is a scene in the movie *Jerry McGuire* that always reminds me of being a recruiter. When Tom Cruise is in the locker room with Cuba Gooding Jr. and he begs him *"help me help you."* Often times I have found myself in what seems to be the same situation with many job seekers: begging them to just listen to me. *I know what I am talking about. If you don't listen you are going to screw this up! And then*

you AND I are both toast! That is what a good recruiter will want to say when someone who has the potential to get hired doesn't *get it*.

Here is how the job placement agency process works: There are two sides to a placement agency: Sales and Recruitment. The sales team scopes out the companies who need to hire personnel and contracts them to use their agency to find qualified personnel. The recruiting agents take it from there.

Recruiting agents get a job description, a salary range, and job requirements from the company in need of hiring employees. They will also receive the information on the company's benefits including:

- PTO (paid time off): holidays, vacation, sick days, personal days and bereavement leave.
- Health care: medical, dental, vision
- Retirement: 401k plan, stock options, pension plan
- Miscellaneous: transit check program, bonus incentive, lunch plan allowance, and whatever other type of compensation given to employees other than annual salary.

The company signs a contract to pay a fee (15% to 25% of the base annual salary) usually 30 days after the start date, with a 90-day guarantee period. In return for agreeing to pay this fee the Employer can:

- Interview an unlimited number of candidates until someone is hired.
- Have a 90-day guarantee to make sure the person is doing the job to their liking and according to the rules and regulations of the company.
- Call off the search at any time with no obligation.

When candidates come in and meet with a recruiter they must provide a resume, take any tests needed to *prove* that they have the necessary job requirements (Excel, PowerPoint, MS Word) and confirm that they will be available to work the days and hours required for the position. They must also pass a criminal background check. NOTE: *If you have anything on your record, even unpaid tickets or a loan default, tell your recruiter. Believe me, it will save you in the long run. I have seen people lose offers because they did not tell anyone about a felony or misdemeanor that they didn't think would show up on the background check. Once it shows up and you never warned anyone about it. So, guess what?* You're finished. *You will not get the job.*

Now, if you use a recruiter, don't be faithful to just one. It is not what you know; *it's who you know*. If you are working with one recruiter great, if you have three, even better. Meet with as many recruiters as possible. And make no mistake about it: meeting with a recruiter is a job interview in itself.

" I am a 25-year-old recent graduate of Harvard College with a degree in French Literature. Finding a job as a twenty-something fresh out of college can be daunting and at times overwhelming process, particularly for those of us with those nebulous humanities titles and broad liberal arts backgrounds (uh, French Literature?). Here, I can't help thinking of the song from Avenue Q, 'What Do You Do With a B.A. in English?':

What do you do with a B.A. in English?
What is my life going to be?
Four years of college and plenty of knowledge
Have earned me this useless degree."

"Certainly, it is easy, and even tempting, to fall into the trap of feeling ill-prepared for the world outside the hallowed grounds of academia. This was no exception for me; when

I first moved to the city, I had absolutely no idea how to go about finding a job. After sending countless emails proclaiming my Imminent Migration to The Big Apple and my Great Search for Employment to friends, and friends of friends, and friends of friends of friends, I came up empty-handed. Frustrated one afternoon, I finally got online and went to craigslist to start searching for job listings.

"Jill had an ad on Craigslist, so I sent my resume to her, and within an hour, I had a new message in my inbox asking me to come in for an interview the following day. Jill sat me down, reviewed my resume, and had a lengthy discussion with me about my background, my resume, my professional and personal interests, what I was looking for, and what I was hoping to accomplish. She took copious notes, opened a file with my name on it, and within a week of that initial meeting, had found me a position at a small reinsurance law firm downtown where I remained happily employed."

-Laurel H.

Using A Recruiter: Pros & Cons

PROS

- **Inside information about the interviewer.**

A good recruiter will tell you what the employer is like both professionally and personally. How do we know? The people who do the hiring at companies are not only our client; many are also our friends. We have had many lunches and dinners together. We have gone to each other's weddings and exchanged gifts when our babies were born. We speak to these people everyday and we don't just discuss job applicants. So I know my clients very well and have so for years.

What do they admire about people they've met and hired in the past? What are the worst things you can do when interviewing with them? This information is invaluable. You can do all the research possible on the company, but you can't research the interviewer's beliefs and feelings. A good recruiter will make you privy to this information. We will not tell you personal things, only the things you should do to make them smile instead of wince on your interview.

- **Feedback**

Anyone working with a recruiter will get feedback on how they interviewed much faster (probably the day of your interview) and the feedback will be useful for any job-seeker. Feedback is crucial in a job search. If you do not get the job, and you have no recruiter, you will have no idea why you weren't hired. The company who met with you is not going to call you and say: "*Hey Dave, we didn't like that you wore a wrinkled shirt and a tie with little red reindeer on it: it's July! Then you nailed your coffin shut when you slipped in that you couldn't work over-time because you love your dog and couldn't leave him alone longer than 8 hours day.*"

When the company does send an e-mail, a note, or calls you back, they will simply say, "*Thank you for coming in, but we are not interested at this time.*" Oh by the way "at this time" means never. In this market, job seekers are lucky if a company gets back to them at all. If the company you interviewed with does not call back for any reason within 10 days, you're toast.

- **No Money Down Ever!**

Some agencies actually charge the job seeker before they are hired. STAY AWAY from them. They are only for people who have jobs and want to find a new one for a lot more money. If you follow the steps of this book you won't need to shell out money to a recruiter. The recruiter will help you for free.

CONS

- **The Finder's Fee**

More companies are recruiting through Internet sites in an attempt to reduce paying agency fees. The companies that do use a recruiter and pay the finder's fee have 90 days to decide if they will keep the new hire. If the company is on the fence about their new hire, they will usually fire that person. Why should the company be out thousands of dollars if their new employee is not showing potential? My point is, they are paying money to get you to work for them. You need to hit the ground running. *(More on that in Chapter 10 Staying Power.)*

- **Control**

You do not get to be in control of this situation. You must listen and do what the recruiter tells you to and quickly. You are in a race with other applicants to get the job. You and your recruiter are a team. The recruiter is the coach and they call the shots. You are the player. You must listen and act and deliver. Time is money. If they ask you to change something about your resume DO IT as soon as you hang up the phone with them and email it to them ASAP. Your recruiter wants to send your resume to a client with the changes as soon as possible before the client moves on to someone else. If you wait and say "I'll fix it tonight" you just lost out. Oh that makes us so mad; getting a revised resume in our inbox two days later and already someone else is at the company for a second interview.
NOTE: *If you are a control freak, move on. Save yourself and the recruiter a headache and get a job on your own.*

- **The Good, The Bad, and The Ugly**

You will hear the good, the bad, and the ugly...maybe that is a Pro. But it could honestly be a con if your recruiter is not a kind person. Be prepared, your recruiter might be a jerk. Problem is, the jerks seem to always have such great clients. Don't you hate that? But stick with them, take their criticisms, act on them and change when you need to. Do not get angry with them. Truth is: they are saying and doing whatever they can to get you hired.

- **Ahhh, *they* will find me a job. I can sit tight and relax.**

Many people wait on their recruiters and stop working on their own to find a job. They put all their eggs in their recruiter's basket. Don't wait. If you have more time to interview and not enough interviews, get more recruiters to work with you. And as I said before you'd better be your own recruiter as well.

Whose Side are they on ANYWAY?

A recruiter is on the job seeker's side *and* their client's side. They have to be, to be a good recruiter and to be successful. But never forget this: *people come and go over the years but clients stay*. The relationship a recruiter has with their client is tight. Don't ever call the client on your own or go over your recruiter's head. You will lose every time. The recruiter will not be happy and neither will the client. They hired a recruiter so they don't have to speak with job applicants all day. Call your recruiter with questions on anything and everything. NOTE: *The only time you should call the company is when your recruiter tells you to call the company.*

If you bomb an interview, but your recruiter has faith in you, they will explain everything you did to blow it (the client called and told them what they thought of you soon after you walked out). But if you don't heed their advice on the next interview, your recruiter probably won't send you out again. Now you are making them look bad. Recruiters do not like that. It is our job to help you get it right. But it is not our desire to fail along with you again and again. If you simply listen and keep *trying* most recruiter's will stay with you until you get a job, especially if you absorb what is written in the remaining chapters.

Jill DeSena-Shook

Chapter Three

RESUME WRITING

FACT: Your resume will be reviewed in **less than 30 seconds** before the employer has decided to delete it or call you for an interview. Usually companies will have a Human Resources department that handles all the interviewing. Managers in HR get hundreds of resumes a day and they are looking for certain, specific things. If they don't see them within 30 seconds they will delete your resume and continue to hunt for a resume that matches their job description.

"When I graduated from Yale, I thought my degree from an Ivy League school would mean job offers would come pouring in and opportunities would just fall in my lap. This was not the case for me, and it was not the case for many of my peers. The job market right now is, at best, competitive. Fortunately, I was a quick study and learned that in order to find a job, I not only had to be proactive, but also had to tailor my resume and how I presented myself to each and every job I applied to. As an early twenty-something fresh out of college, I learned that I had to be rather shortsighted when telling potential employers about my goals/ambitions. No one wants to hire someone that they honestly think they're going to have to replace in the next year or two. I learned that resume editing is of the UTMOST importance. I always thought that since I had accomplished a lot, the one-page rule didn't apply to me. I was, in fact, wrong."
-Jason R.

MATCH YOUR RESUME WITH THE JOB DESCRIPTION

When employers are sifting through hundreds of resumes for one job opening, they look for two things: first, JOB EXPERIENCE and second, DEGREES and CERTIFICATIONS. The JOB EXPERIENCE must match the job description in order for you to be considered for an interview. Otherwise your resume will end up in the trash.

You must understand that this process is not about the YOU. It is about the JOB. In those 30 seconds, the person reviewing your resume is only concerned with filling their job opening, *and* ***not*** *with learning about you*. They don't care about you until you start working for them. The resume review process and the interview are about what you can do for the company. If your resume is all about you, your senior thesis, your fraternity/sorority, and your study abroad program, they will probably delete it. There are valuable skills demonstrated from your experience, but do they cater to the job description?

Constantly Changing
A resume is a fluid document that changes constantly to fit the description of whatever job you are applying for. Do not EVER lie, but use whatever experience you do have to fit with the job description in some way, shape, or form.

When your resume displays skills and experiences that *relate* to the job it will have a better chance of getting called for an interview. You will know what is required for the job from the job description in the advertisement. The person reviewing resumes is trying to match resumes with the certain job description. If the skills match, they will then check to see if the experience level and educational requirements are met. Then they will call you in for an interview.

For example, when hiring an administrative assistant, employers are looking for the resumes that actually HAVE ADMINISTRATIVE DUTIES LISTED ON THEM. Such as answering phones; faxing; filing; travel arrangements; Fed-Ex; typing; customer liaison. Even if a person has never had the title of an administrative assistant, most job experiences can be tailored to highlight the ability to answer phones, file, type, deal with customers and MULTI-TASK.

But My Experience Doesn't Match

If you cannot, no matter how hard you try, find anything in your background that matches or fits the job description, then guess what? You should **not** be applying for that job. Do not send your resume to that company for that job opening. It will be deleted. And worse—when a position opens up at that same company and you are a perfect match, and you send your resume again, they may recognize your name and delete it again. Why? They already saw your name before and may feel that you are just randomly sending out your resume for any opening. *You will risk loosing credibility by sending your standard resume to any open position without tailoring it to the job description.*

HOW TO FORMAT AND WRITE YOUR RESUME

Length: The One-Page Rule

Unless you have over ten years of experience your resume should be *one page long.* Even with years of experience, try to keep it to one page. There are only certain professions and positions in which a detailed work history requires more than one page on a resume. You're not there yet.

Formatting

Please style your resume using MS Word document format. If you use a Mac, make sure that it will be formatted correctly when opened as an MS Word or a PDF document. If a company, including a recruiter, cannot open it, they will delete it. If they can, this will also *prove* that you know how to construct a document using MS Word correctly. You might say that you know MS Word very well, but if your resume is not formatted correctly, they *know* you are lying.

Fonts, Font Size, and Styling

Do not use weird fonts with lots of bold, italics and underlining everywhere. Use **Times New Roman** or **Century** font styles or something that looks like the writing from a newspaper article. Do not use letters that are too small or too large: Font size 12 is perfect.

The following was provided from the Human Resources Hiring Manager of a large Hedge Fund in New York City:

- *You will be judged on your resume. Any format, grammatical, spelling, or style error/ inconsistency will disqualify you. Highly qualified candidates have lost interview slots simply because they presented themselves poorly on paper due to a missed comma or period, or misaligned bullet points.*

- *If you allow your recruiting agent to use their company masthead at the start of your resume, consider how it will alter your format and pagination. Failure to submit a properly formatted resume, regardless of reason, WILL count against you. Take charge of your own recruiting process and have the insight to review anything that is sent out under your name. Your recruiter may not be an expert in word processing. Don't rely on him or her. YOU should be an expert in that area, so make sure it shows. If you are concerned, only put PDF versions of your resume out there.*

- *Do not submit or bring a resume that is not up-to-date. If you need an extra day to update your resume, take it. Don't allow your recruiter to send over a resume in DRAFT form: I will compare the versions, and spelling or grammatical errors even on DRAFT resumes do count.*

- *If you submit a resume in a word processing document, I WILL "unhide" all formatting, check the character spacing, use of tabs, tables, carriage returns, and prior changes. Make sure that your resume not only looks good, but that it illustrates your word-processing skills.*

One last formatting and style rule: Do not put a picture of yourself on your resume. Do not put any color or graphics, phrases or quotes of any kind on your resume, either. I can tell you from experience that employers and recruiters view those "extras" as tacky distractions. It actually makes most of us laugh, and then we delete it. Once again, this is not about you it is about what you can do. At the end of this Chapter, you can find examples of properly formatted and appropriate resumes.

Below (on the next pages), you will be given key information on how to present yourself in the process of preparing information for potential employers, as well as a sense of the means and the objectives to move ahead, to get hired and to keep that job!

PERSONAL INFORMATION

Name
ALWAYS AT THE TOP; ALWAYS FRONT AND CENTER. (To achieve this make sure you use the center alignment function, NOT the tab button). Usually a font size of 16 to 20 works best. Your name should stand out a bit. So you can use a bold font if you like.

E-mail
In this day and age, your e-mail address should go directly underneath your name. If you are submitting your resume in a word document, make sure the e-mail address is "hyper-linked" (the font will become blue and the address underlined). A simple click on your e-mail address will allow your prospective employer to respond to you quickly. You just put yourself on speed-dial.

Address
This information can either be at the top or at the very bottom; this is your choice. But this choice should *not* be based on your personal preferences. Understand that something as simple as where you live (and where you decide to place your address on your resume) may very well affect your chances of getting an interview. *Be aware* of how your address may be perceived by others and that you may be judged by it. Here's why....

If you live far away from the office, some employers might discard your resume without looking past your address. Without even seeing your qualifications, they just decided for you that the commute is too long and you'd probably often be late and miss too many days. Also, if you live in the "bad" part of town, this may hinder you as well because of the stereotypes associated with your neighborhood. In these situations, you might consider putting your address at the end.

On the flip side, if you live two to ten miles from the office, it may help you get the interview. Employers like to hire people who live near the office. Most days you will not be tardy and won't mind staying later if need be. So if you live close by then consider putting it at the top.

Phone Number (preferably a cell)
Whether you provide a cell or home number on your resume, *be aware* of your voicemail greeting. If your voicemail comes on and there is a personal greeting with your voice saying: *"Hey all you sexy mammas and papas! I ain't at 'ome so leave me a message at da' tone and I will call you back when I get 'ome,"* **DELETE IT.** Instead, leave a professional sounding voicemail greeting so that if a company calls you for an interview they won't change their mind and hang up! What is wrong with some people? I cannot tell you how many times have I called an entry-level job-seeker and heard something like Beyonce's "All the Single Ladies" song on a answering machine. I am calling from my office, in the middle of a workday to set up an interview with a huge company and I have to listen to a full minute of *"Uu-uu-ohhhh! If yah like it, then yah should'ah put'ah ring on it."* Spare us! Think about how you are showing yourself. <u>You</u> listed that number on your resume. *Come on!*

Try this instead:
"Thank you for calling Jeff's voice mail. I am not able to receive your call at the moment but if you would kindly leave your name and telephone number, I will call you back as soon as I receive your message. Have a nice day."

With a voice mail message this considerate, I would surly leave a message and not just hang up because no one answered. And I would try to be just as kind back in my reply.

I do not like when people say "I will call you back at my earliest convenience" on their voice-mail message.

Why? Well, I called *them* for a job to help *them*. Why do I have to wait for them to call me at a time that is convenient for *them*. I have a job I need to fill. I want to know that I am a priority. I would like to hear the words "I will return your call as soon as I can" or "right away." This way I know they are interested in speaking to me with *me* in mind not themselves and what is convenient for them.

Your voice mail message may be the first impression an employer gets of you. Make it considerate, attentive and also kind. You are doing yourself a severe disservice if you don't.

Your "Friends" and Your Voice Mail

Some friends your age will hear your new message and say: "Hey, what's up? Good professional message, buddy; good luck with the job search. Anyway..." Keep those friends close and share contacts with them in your job search. Help each other. And while you search, it is good to have a friend to talk to that knows what you are going through. Some days it will be crucial for your self esteem. Other days you will need to give them help and advice. Saying the words "It's going to be okay. Someone will hire you soon, just keep at it" to a friend enforces it to yourself as well. Network with people who are job searching also not just with people who have jobs already.

Now if a friend leaves a message on your new voice mail that says: "What a tool! What kind of loser-businessman message was that, you jackass?," distance yourself from them. They are going nowhere fast. In three years, you will have nothing in common with them. In ten years, you won't even know their telephone number. Why? Maybe *they* are losers. If you are someone reading this who would leave a message like that on your friend's voice mail to bust on them, grow up. Don't end up a loser. (You know who you are).

OBJECTIVE

Guess what? Employers don't care what your OBJECTIVE is *unless it matches the exact job they are trying to fill*. An OBJECTIVE can only pigeonhole you into one type of job. An employer will not consider you to be a marketing assistant if your OBJECTIVE says "human-resources coordinator." And guess what! You might actually want that job as a marketing assistant with that company. Your objective is to get hired and earn a paycheck. So ***you need to change your objective EVERY time you send out a resume and adjust it according to the job title of the position you are applying for. This will stand out to the employer and they will read it and think "OK, here we go! This person wants to be an administrative assistant. Great!" They will read on.***

Education

- Put EDUCATION first if you are a recent college graduate and last if you have held a full-time job for at least two years (in this case, your WORK EXPERIENCE goes first). If you worked part-time while going to school, put EDUCATION first.

- List your school.
- Include your GPA (Grade Point Average) *only if* you have ABOVE a 3.0
- List your major and your minor & the year of graduation.
- If you did not finish your degree, write down what credits have been earned toward the degree. If you are still in school and finishing up at night, then write: anticipated graduation 2011 (or whatever year you will be finished).
- If you have never gone to college, then write the high school that you graduated from. If you do not have a high school diploma, then do not list EDUCATION at all.

Skills

- List all the computer programs you are **proficient** in. This means the programs that you can use *proficiently* at a job that someone is PAYING YOU TO DO.
- List your SKILLS in bullet form *after* your WORK EXPERIENCE portion. List your typing speed if it is over 50 words per minute.
- If you speak a language fluently put it down. If you took Spanish in high school and you can ask where the *cuarto de baño* is and that is pretty much it, *don't* write Spanish. Sometimes people list "moderate Spanish." That is ridiculous. Would you write moderate English on your resume? Either you can work in a job speaking Spanish to people who speak Spanish or you can't.

NOTE: Make sure you stick these skills into your WORK EXPERIENCE bullets (this *proves* you used the programs in your job tasks)

Example for PowerPoint:

- *Created PowerPoint slideshows for 3+ presentations weekly for the marketing department's account proposals.*

Interests / Activities

- Put interests and activities at the very bottom of your resume. Again, do *not* go onto a second page.
- This includes: any musical instrument, sports you played in school, study-abroad programs and any public service of any kind. (YES, even Boy Scouts and Girl Scouts but only if you continued with it thoughout high school or college.) This shows you are "well rounded."

**These things will not GET you an interview, but they may help strike up conversation during the interview.*

For Example:

Interests & Activities

- State University Soccer Team: 4 years
- Alpha Beta Alpha Fraternity: Chapter Vice President, 2008/2009
- Lead Trombone, State University Marching Band: 4 years
- Big Siblings Organization of Boston MA: Volunteer since 2004

References available upon request

Yeah? No kidding. This line is a waste of valuable space on a resume. It is understood that you will give references. If you don't and they are required, guess what? Right! You don't get the offer.

NOTE: Do not offer references during an interview. Wait until someone asks for them. And *never* send a letter of recommendation along with a resume to a company. If I am interviewing someone and they pull out references or letters of recommendation that I never asked for, it annoys me. I asked my clients and it annoys them as well. It seems that the person being interviewed is either trying to hide something or they are just desperate. They pulled out these letters out to say: "See! I am good I have a letter that says so."

"An offered letter of recommendation is that reliable. It is possible the letter was written under duress or out of pity. If I have something in writing, I am going to call them anyway, so the letter is a waste. All I really want is current contact information for previous supervisors."
-Keith J. (Director of a Private Equity Firm)

Work experience
"I don't care if they worked at a grocery store. I did when I was in school. But they have to show that they are a worker, that they have held down jobs and went in everyday. School is never enough nowadays. I want them to explain their job and have the intelligence to know that a job is a job, as long as you do it well."
-Vince M. (Director of Human Resources at a global law firm)

The Importance of Multi-Tasking
Whether you are Donald Trump or a waiter, the common thread in your job is multi-tasking. Use that to your advantage. Whether your job experience is as a lawyer, a construction worker, a bartender, a secretary, a lifeguard, or a CEO, you are still a multi-tasker. So no matter what you have done in your life, you can make a terrific resume and *show* yourself to be a competent worker. But remember a waiter does not have the same experience as "The Donald."

THE MULTI-TASKING FORMULA

This formula is tried and true to use for work experience. Follow this simple formula when listing your job descriptions/skills:

Formula For Each Bullet in Work Experience

VERB + NUMBER + TIME FRAME = *MULTI-TASKING*

Example:

- *Collected 100+ resumes* weekly

Go A Step Further:

- Collected and logged 100+ resumes weekly for 10 managers in a 25+ employee placement agency

*Now we know how big the company is that you worked for, how many resumes came in each week, and how many managers you assist within that company. We know how busy you were, how big the company was, and how much you worked.

There is a structure to this process of having your resume make use of this specificity. It takes seriously:
VERB+NUMBER+TIME FRAME=MULTI-TASKING.

VERBS (Some to Start With):

Answered
Arranged
Collected
Composed
Controlled
Created
Developed
Directed
Distributed
Educated
Fashioned
Implemented
Investigated
Maintained
Ordered
Organized
Planned
Prepared
Produced
Researched
Studied
Tracked
Trained
Typed

+NUMBERS:

- *How much?* or *How many?* will explain *in numbers* the size of the company, job, task, etc.
- How much money?
- How many clients, calls, supplies, data, deliveries, etc.?

+TIME FRAME:

- *How many times a day? week? month? year?* will explain what was expected of you day to day, week to week.
- Indicate what was expected of you during "down-time" as well. (This shows you can prepare for the up-winds in business.)
- List what projects or reports you were responsible for on a monthly or annual basis.

Demonstrate Your Experience in Bullet Form (Include Your Skills)

- Maintained a Microsoft Outlook database of over 12,000 clients on a weekly basis.
- Supervised 3 bar-tenders nightly: serving over 600 drinks.
- Answered a 10-line phone system for over 30 people; accepting and directing over 100 calls daily.
- Entered 10 to 20 appointments and cancelations in office database system daily.
- Organized files and documents for over 1200 patients in a month-long project to restructure office-filing system.
- Accepted, tracked, and sent 40+ Priority Fed-Ex packages weekly for principal managers and staff.
- Managed and trained staff of 5 to create over 37 different types of drinks for over 100 customers daily.
- Typed and proofread 7+ documents a day for an assistant manager and two supervisors.

Questions to define these ideas

Let's say you worked at a grocery store:
What is the name of the store?
During what time frame did you work at the store?
How big was the store? How many locations in the state?

How much revenue does this chain take in?
How many people did you check out each day and for how many hours a day?
How many bags did you pack?
How much money did you handle in your drawer that you were responsible for?
Did you deduct coupons each shift? How much and how many?
Did you do cash drops or reconcile your drawer at the end of each shift?

Example of this framework for applying these ideas

Price Chopper Supermarket
June 2006 to August 2008
Check-out Clerk for a large supermarket chain with over 5,000 customers weekly.

- Scanned over 2000+ food and grocery items every 8 to 12 hour shift.
- Developed a concise method of scanning and bagging items for the fastest service.
- Maintained a balanced draw of over $3500+ in cash and checks each shift.
- Organized $100+ worth of coupon savings and store credits each shift.
- Loaded cars with over 300+ packages a day for customers, maintaining with a smile excellent service at our store.

But if you write this:
Piggly Wiggly Supermarket
June of 2008 to August 2008
Cashier

- Scanned food items
- Bagged groceries
- Collected Money

...Yep, I would delete that faster than you can say "Piggly Wiggly."

Yes—that is right—you can make that job as a checkout clerk job look pretty good if you apply this formula. The person reading your resume WILL be impressed.

Matching Your Experience
Do you know how many people I meet who have experience doing the jobs listed below and they leave it off their resume! Every time that I ask why, they say, "Well it didn't apply to the job I want to get." So they listed their *thesis* on their resume instead! Come on?! No one cares about your thesis, but guess what they do care about? They care if you have WORKED before. Right! You know why? Because that is what they need you to do: WORK.

Below (on the next page), view the common jobs that should be listed on your resume for most entry-level positions at most companies in most industries. Some jobs will obviously require specific training and qualifications to begin in even an entry-level position, but most other entry-level jobs do not. Most entry-level positions are administrative in some way. You need to use this to your advantage.

An array of job possibilities:

Bank Teller
Bar Back
Bartender
Bus Boy / Girl
Camp Counselor
Car Detailer
Cashier
Child Care Worker
Clothing Sales
College Lab Tech
Construction Worker
Cosmetic Sales
Deli Counter Clerk
Department Store Sales
Dishwasher
Fast Food Worker
File Clerk
Gas Station Attendant
Hostess
Landscaper
Library Aid
Lifeguard
Maintenance Worker
Newspaper Delivery
Pizza Delivery
Receptionist
Short Order Cook
Truck Driver
Tutor
Waiter/Waitress

Being a waiter is difficult: you have a million things to remember, while paying close attention to details. You have to serve with a kind disposition when you might have a splitting headache and sore feet. Child Care? Anyone who has taken care of *one* child knows that you can't even go to the bathroom and take your time!

These jobs allow you to show how busy you were, while demonstrating an understanding that every job has down time. On your resume, have bullets that list what your tasks were while you were busy and while your job was slow. This demonstrates an understanding that you are used to the ups and downs of daily business. Use the multi-tasking formula and recall exactly what you did hour-by-hour, shift-by-shift, weekly, and monthly and explain it in your bullets on your resume.

Own Your Job Experience

Don't discredit yourself because you were a library aid. It is a job! It deals with both adults and children, coming and going, hour by hour. These people not only need help, but they leave the library a mess. This job involves the filing of numerous books and papers and the logging of data on the computer. It requires patience and kindness. It takes an individual who knows how to speak quietly and calmly and maintain a visual poise about themselves. It takes stamina to remain at a job that seems monotonous day after day. If you did it, then show it all in your bullets. Own that job! Recognize it; acknowledge it; appreciate it! And appreciate yourself in this! This is not being haughty; it is appreciating what you put into that job and how it had its own value for you—whatever the social image you think it might imply! Appreciate the reality beyond the image!

The point is, don't ever say, "Oh! I just worked at the McKing's drive through window" and not put it on your resume. I have been at a fast-food drive-through window on a Friday night. I have seen those cashiers behind the window and it is no joke. Those people are busy! Watch when a customer has to get out of their car and come into the restaurant because something was missing from their order. There is no room for error. When you get yelled at, even just once, *you try as hard as possible never to have that happen again*. The same thing applies with a cook or a bartender or gas station attendant. Have you ever seen all the little tasks these employees are able to complete as fast as they can, over and over again?

That is work experience with the public, and it is extremely important to put on your resume. Unite this experience with a degree *in your resume* and show yourself to be a multi-tasker who can work hard, think, problem solve and deliver. Bravo! That is what employers are searching for when they view a resume: someone who can **deliver results**.

Your multi-tasking bullets should *show* the fact that you know how to deliver. Whatever is on that resume is going to be what you discus on the interview. If you worked as a landscaper and worked so hard every summer that your bones hurt when you got home - you will *prove* it in the way you talk about the job.

Military Service in the Armed Forces

Believe it or not, there have been several instances where I have interviewed individuals with military experience, and it is not listed anywhere on their resume. Most times I hear, "Well it doesn't really apply" or "It was just ROTC" or "I don't want to work in the military anymore." WHAT?! Are you people nuts? If you have ANY military experience—boot camp, ROTC, Reserves or National Guard, let alone active duty—it is something you OWN; it is your experience. Write the things you did each day that ordinary people DO NOT.

For example:

- Awoke at 5 am each morning, 6 days a week, to begin training.
- Maintained a disciplined daily regimen in order to perfect the element of teamwork.
- *Cleaned and folded underwear to maintain a 4x4 inch square of white cotton in personal footlocker.*

For those of you who have been there, you know that there are a million different bullet points that could be written from your basic training alone. Use bullets that describe what life was like day-to-day. Those are the bullets we will be impressed with. They are truth staring us in the face.

Military experience is seen as reliable. You have *proven* to have discipline like no one else. Employers are going to have a prejudice of you that includes believing you will be on time for work and try your best. You were TRAINED that way. That is what we think when we see "military service" on a resume.

Slow As Sugar Honey Iced Tea

When I encounter people who don't like to MOVE, I can first see it from their resume. On most occasions, I don't even bother calling them in to meet with me. I immediately know that they don't like to move their fingers or their legs (or their minds) too much. It is actually visible on their resume. All the white space on it and the simplicity of the resume screams "LAZY." They do the minimum amount of work they HAVE TO DO. They don't get IT. They might never get IT. I can't waste time with them. If your resume looks like the first one included here, wise up and start moving.

Be Meticulous about a Resume

Your resume is an exam that determines if you move up or get left back. It is graded but this time the grade is PASS / FAIL. Make sure every thing is perfect. That's right! Make it PERFECT. Do not **overload** your resume with the bullets and wording; your resume needs to be ONE PAGE. So be concise and effective in the space that you have available.

"People our age might have a hard time imagining that things as small as the placement of a single comma in our resume, or how much we chat with the receptionist before an interview matter—but they do. From the second we walk into the building, there is the possibility of being noticed, and judged, by someone who will have a say in whether or not the job is ours. ***All of the little details matter****, and unfortunately, if you don't pay attention to them, the employer might find someone else for the job who does."*
-Travis J.

"With regard to your resume, start out with listening to your recruiter. This is definitely a must-do. *I found Jill's guidance very helpful. (It clearly reduced the amount of time it actually took me to find the right position.) For example, she had recommended that I list the equipment I worked with at JPMorgan and Goldman Sachs. I always had listed my job functions, but never the equipment I worked with. I added these to my resume and I believe it helped to highlight the technical experience I had.*

"Also make sure your resume is properly formatted and spell-checked. Don't rely on MSWord's spell-checker, read and re-read your resume word-for-word to make sure spelling, grammar and formatting is correct and concise."
-Gregory S.

"Having gone through the job hunt process for several months without any results many people start to get discouraged. It's amazing how just a few details can really change the outcome of sending out resumes and never hearing back from companies, to setting up second and third interviews, and getting job offers. My resume had a good amount of work experience, but not enough that it would get me the job I dreamed of. By being able to present my abilities in a much more appropriate manner I noticed that more and more I was hearing back from employers wanting to set up interviews."
-Robert M.

And now, looking at the forms of a Resume
What might a resume look like? See the next pages: each sample resume is on *one* page (with room to spare). And yet, we will see differences in style and in how helpful the resume we are looking at turns out to be.

Jane Miller
jmiller@thisaddress.com

Education
BA in English, GPA 3.3
University of Talley, May 2008

Work Experience
Bank Teller / Federal Savings Bank Mills Place
Part time 2004 to present

- Assisted customers with all banking transactions
- Organized receipts and checks
- Logged transactions and balanced draw
- Maintained good relations with customers

Lifeguard / Mills Place Town Pool
(Summers 1999 to 2008)

- Viewed children and adults in town pool.
- Maintained a safe swimming environment for swimmers.

Skills
MS Word Office Suite
Typing of 65 words per minute

Interests
Swimming, Reading, Golf and Chess

References Available Upon Request

Comments on this rather brief Resume
Jane Miller! Your resume is a "DELETE" if I ever saw one. And it is a shame. You are smart (college grad with a 3.3 average), you can type (65 words per minute), you know MS Word, Excel, and Power Point (MS Office Suite), and you worked all through college (Bank Teller/ Lifeguard). But this resume proves that you do the minimum amount of work possible OR you never really owned any job you had.

Now we are going to make it look like a keeper.

In addition, I have included the resumes of a few other recent college graduates. When my clients saw these first-rate resumes, the applicants got called in for interviews...ASAP. The names, workplaces, and schools have been fictionalized, but the format and bullet-points are the same. They were all hired.

Jane Miller
jmiller@thisaddress.com

Education
Bachelor of the Arts degree in English, GPA 3.3 cum laude
University of Talley, May 2008

Work Experience

Bank Teller / Federal Savings Bank Mills Place
Part-time September 2004 to Present

- Assisted 50 to 100+ customers with savings deposits up to $50K, check cashing up to $10K, opening money market and other accounts each shift.
- Organized all checks and deposits or withdrawal tickets for every transaction with precise dollar amount figures to the penny.
- Maintained good relations with customers and delivered fast, accurate service to clear banking lines as quickly as possible during lunch crowd.
- Created and prepared *Excel* spreadsheets for two banking managers and one supervisor with detailed information on all transactions listed for five tellers daily.
- Answered phone calls for all incoming customer questions and concerns regarding balance, transfers and electronic deposits while maintaining excellent customer service.

Lifeguard / Mills Place Community Pool & Country Club
(Summers 1999 to 2008)

- Lifeguard for town pool with members of over 700 children and adults.
- Maintained a safe swimming environment for swimmers.
- Checked passes and updated member registration for over 100 people daily during summertime hours of 9 am to 6 pm.
- Collected money and provided receipts for anyone without ID for town pool.
- Laundered and folded 75+ towels in locker rooms after closing.
- Cleaned bathrooms and tile floors to maintain flawless condition of club.
- Responsible for Lost & Found items for members.
- Fully trained and certified in CPR, First Aid, and Water Rescue Skills

Skills

Proficient usage of MS Office applications, with superior knowledge of MS Word
Typing of 65 words per minute

Interests & Activities
Swim Team: University of Talley 4 years
Reigning Chess Champion of Rhode Island State: 2003 to 2006

Julie Winter
jwinter@thenet.com

Education
Bachelor of Science, Mass Communications, Commonwealth University, 2006

Employment History

Account Coordinator, Product Code Inc.
February 2002-Present

- Collaborated with clients on editorial revisions and distribution of feature releases.
- Performed administrative duties for company president and two account executives such as: telephone coverage, typing letters, Fed-Ex sending and tracking, as well as client liaison.

Internship Honahan, Klein & Hanson LLP
July 2005-January 2006

- Create and revise legal documents using *Microsoft Word 2003*
- Coordinate meetings, conferences and appointments using Outlook.
- Arranged travel arrangements both foreign and domestic for any travel for a litigation department of 16 employees.
- Process time records, expense reports and billing documents for 40 to 90 billable hours weekly for two attorneys.
- Answer telephone calls promptly and direct calls appropriately for a 22-partner firm.

Temporary Assistant, Silver Staffing Services
February 2001-February 2002

Legal Assistant, City Group Insurance Companies

- Supported legal staff with high-volume filing, photocopying and faxing.
- Designed and organized new filing systems for over 1200 cases and reports.

Sales Assistant, Farrall Publishing

- Maintained advertising accounts for daily and weekly trade publications.
- Typeset and proofread advertisements into AdBooker publishing software.

Event Coordinator, JCD Business Media/Expositions

- Registered exhibitors and retailers for *Giftware Business* trade show.
- Assigned 50+ booth locations, coordinated equipment rentals and sold advertising.

Assistant Sales Clerk, Jenner Michaels Designs
November 1999-February 2001

- Serviced over 100+ customers daily in a busy upscale clothing store.
- Performed administrative duties for two managers including phone coverage and ordering supplies for store.
- Organized all garments by steaming, hanging and folding hundreds of articles each shift.

Related Skills
Strong Microsoft Word; Lexis-Nexis; Outlook, typing speed 75 wpm

Nicole Barr
nbarr@thisaddress.com

Education:
The O'Brian State University (with the Study Abroad Program at The American College Dublin, College of the Liberal Art)
Political Science Major, History Minor, Spring 2005

Experience:
New York State Executive Department, Division of Human Rights
Intern, Summer 2004
Directed plaintiff and defendant settlement meetings for anti-discrimination and human rights law cases
Prepared case files, including the formation of final case decisions
Interviewed witnesses, plaintiffs, and defendants
Conducted field visits as division representative

State College Area Family YMCA
Instructor, November 2005-present
Supervised after-school program for 75- 80 children daily
Planned and executed array of programs for all members and created a family atmosphere

Hempstead Golf and Country Club
Waitress, Summer 2003, 2004, 2005
Member of wait staff in charge of an eight-table station five nights a week.
Member of planning team for activities, carnivals and client meetings for over 700 members

Quinn Co. Insurance Company
Office Assistant, December 2001-August 2002, December 2003
Prepared and processed invoices, memos and completed attorney worksheets for three associates
Answered a 12-line phone switchboard and directed calls to 50+ employees.
Assisted other office workers in the maintenance of case-work and delivery of court documents.

Skills:
Typing of 70 words per minute
Proficient in MS Word, MS Excel, MS PowerPoint, Internet Research

Activities/Honors:
President, O'Brian University Club Soccer Team, January 2004- January 2006
Created and managed team schedule and budget, designed and conducted team try-outs, practices and tournaments, created all travel arrangements, managed and coached other players during competitions
Dancer, O'Brian University Marathon, February 2006
Participated in 48-hour dance marathon benefiting pediatric cancer treatment and research, which raised over $4 million
Chair, O'Brian University Dance Marathon, 2003-2004
Organized and managed fundraising events, coordinated between soccer team and organizations to raise funds and plan activities
Team Member, O'Brian University Club Soccer, 2002-2006
International Baccalaureate Degree, South Side High School

Hayden Summer
summerh@thenet.com

File-Scope Corporation, New York, NY, 2002-current
Administrative Associate and Productions Associate

- Provided comprehensive administrative support to the Productions Supervisor
- Created invoice reports using Microsoft Excel for a 25+ staff weekly
- Liaised with the bookkeeper, shipping personnel, suppliers, and sales people
- Coordinated, scheduled, and maintained calendar and itinerary schedules; scheduled meetings and conferences, tracked attendance and vacation schedules
- Answered a multi-line phone system, forwarded and screened calls as needed
- Organized special events: annual holiday party, and lunch celebrations
- Sorted and filed e-mail records for three main departments
- Tracked shipments and monitored urgent Fed-Ex mail, 10 to 20 packages weekly
- Ordered and maintained the office supply inventory; worked closely with vendors
- Supervised repairs and maintenance of office equipment/facility: computer and phone wiring
- Acted as a liaison between customers, subsidiaries and partners
- Followed up on cash balances; transfer of funds or loans from/to mill customers
- Supported accounting department to resolve customer litigations
- Recovered overdue invoices

Beyond Vintage School of Design, New York, New York, 2000-2002
Registrar Assistant and Secretary

- Sorted and filed records for over 1500+ student records
- Organized and issued envelops for all report cards for students using Microsoft Word
- Created Microsoft Excel spreadsheets to maintain all accounts payable information
- Coordinated, scheduled, and maintained calendar and itinerary schedules quarterly

EDUCATION

- B.M. in classical piano performance in the ABC School of Music in New York, New York (2002-2005)
- Artists Diploma in musicology and classical piano performance at Oberlin College in Oberlin, Ohio (1999-2000)
- Class Valedictorian (19967-1999)

SKILLS

Microsoft Word, Microsoft Excel, PowerPoint, Microsoft Outlook

Hayley Springs
springsh@thenet.com

Education
Drummond University, Philadelphia, PA
B.A. in International Area Studies, Graduated September 2007, 3.8 GPA

Work Experience
International Professional Association Internship, New York, NY
Administrative Assistant, May to August 2008

- Provided telephone coverage of four phone lines for attorneys
- Performed research as assigned for a team of three attorneys
- Maintained internal case-tracking system for over 200 cases
- Created a timeline to track the status of over 150 cases to ensure progress
- Managed specific deadlines for all departmental cases
- Responsible for client correspondence including, but not limited to, writing letters, sending facsimiles, and sending emails
- Organized and conducted review of all incoming documentation necessary for all cases within the department
- Utilized Microsoft Outlook to stay in constant and rapid contact with clients regarding matters of their respective cases

The Perfect PourNew York, NY
Wine Specialist and Sales Associate, January 2006 to May 2008

- Handled customer inquiries regarding over 40 kinds of fine wine and 15 to 20 craft beers
- Administered wine tastings to over 100+ patrons each night
- Organized and booked talent for weekend shows in the theater room

SH Virtual Business, Madrid, Spain
Marketing Intern and Office Assistant, September to December 2005

- Performed secretarial duties as assigned, all typing and phone coverage for 5 managers
- Conducted market research for designer clothing companies
- Created marketing and sales spreadsheets and presentations for weekly meeting using *Excel* and *PowerPoint*

Learning Systems International, Inc., Washington, D.C.
Training/ Marketing Intern and Assistant, August 2004 to March 2005

- Performed market research to identify possible job opportunities
- Reviewed resumes and conducted initial interviews for potential employees
- Improved hiring methods and procedures
- Edited instruction guides before being released to clients
- Performed secretarial duties as assigned

Skills

- Written and spoken fluency in Spanish
- Typing at 80 WPM
- Proficient usage of MS Office, with superior knowledge of MS Word

Tyler M. Roth
tmroth@thisaddress.com

Education:
C.Feilds University School of Law, New York, New York
J.D. Candidate, Evening Division, May 2009, G.P.A.: 3.07

College of Massachusetts, Worcester, Massachusetts
B.A. in Political Science and Religious Studies with a Concentration in Asian Studies, May 2003, G.P.A.: 3.49
Honors: recipient of Fulbright Research Grant, Sri Lanka; Theta Alpha Kappa National Honor Society; Society for Religious Studies; Pi Sigma Alpha National Honor Society for Political Science
Dean's List (six of eight semesters)
Activities: Men's Varsity Soccer; Founder of the College of Massachusetts Meditation Society

Experience:
Camaj & Corley LLP, Yorktown CT
Summer Associate, May – August 2008
Performed research and drafted legal memoranda on a broad range of litigation issues.
Conducted a fifty-state regulatory survey to the satisfaction of a large corporate client.
Participated in training sessions focused on trial skills.

Hamilton & Chessnut , New York, New York
Assistant to the Chief Corporate Knowledge Counsel, March-May 2008
- Assisted in firm's knowledge management for corporate legal matters.
- Tracked developments in company mergers and acquisitions with extensive research, initial public offerings and private equity investments.

Office of The Department of State New York, New York
Law Clerk, September 2006-February 2008
- Assisted in all phases of small business and personal injury litigation.
- Drafted pleadings, motions and discovery responses.

Shipman Interiors Inc., Coopertown, New York
Project Manager for General Building Contractor, October 2004-August 2006
- Prepared, reviewed and negotiated contracts with subcontractors and project owners for annual sales of $250,000+
- Managed and performed company interface with project architects and owners.

Verizon Communications, Inc., Washington, District of Columbia
Intern for the Vice President of Federal Government Relations, Summer 2001, Summer 2002
- Monitored legislative and regulatory activity in federal telecommunications policy.
- Drafted briefs for witnesses at Congressional hearings.

Skills
Microsoft Office 2003, Outlook, Lexis-Nexis, typing of 65 words per minute

Chapter Four

PROFESSIONAL APPEARANCE

Many of you are not going to like what I am about to say, but it is one of the biggest issues that I have with the younger generations. Your appearance on an interview is the same as your resume: it is not about YOU. This is not the time to express your identity. The interview is about demonstrating what *you can do for the company*. The first step in demonstrating this is to create a professional appearance. There should be NOTHING about your appearance (i.e., clothes, hairstyle, piercings, make-up, tattoos, or heavy cologne) that a corporate professional would or *could* find inappropriate. This is where you can exercise control, and *you had better take every opportunity to look the best you've ever looked on an interview.*

> ***TRUE STORY #1***
> One Friday afternoon, I took a call from a well-known Manhattan attorney. I had placed a secretary in a "temp to perm" position with him. "I want to hire your temp," he said.
>
> "Great!" I said. She had been there three weeks and I guess she proved herself.
>
> "Yes! She is amazing, Jill. She takes "steno" faster than anyone I have ever met and she is a terrific secretary as well. BUT..."
>
> "Uh-oh", I thought.
>
> "Ahh...well, you have to tell her to wax her upper lip or I can't hire her," he stammered. Stunned, I said nothing and keep listening.
>
> "Yeah, I don't know if you've noticed, but her mustache is thicker than mine. She needs to get rid of it. You need to tell her. I don't want to risk losing her...but that cat under her nose is really distracting," he said.
>
> Ouch. I told him that I would speak to her. He was relieved, but before he hung up, he made a point of telling me that I should refrain from telling her that he mentioned this: "This conversation never happened."
>
> When she came into my office to pick up her paycheck, let me tell you, I was more embarrassed than she was after I told her. I started by explaining that so many women got their upper lip waxed. I told her that she was beautiful (which she was) and if she was to achieve getting a permanent job with that company, she would need to present herself as polished as possible. I explained how much more elegant she would look and feel if she did what so many of other women do and got a lip wax. I spoke to her as a concerned friend and explained how easy it was. She did it and was hired a week later. Although I presented it with some TLC, it required the cold hard truth to get her to wax that "cat" and get the job.

For examples on how to look and speak just turn on ABC, CBS or NBC and watch the newscasters: they are a perfect example to follow. Major network newscasters come in all shapes and sizes. They are all different races and ages. They are all dressed beautifully. They are polished and professional. They have to be in order for us to listen to them and find what they are saying to be credible. We are not *distracted* by anything they are wearing or their hairstyle and are completely focused on what they are saying. Plus, we believe them to be a credible source. Dressing meticulously and being polished is powerful.

Department store runs sales on shoes and suits. You don't have to spend a lot of money to get one new suit, a nice pair of shoes and a good haircut. You bought the iPod you wanted. You just got a new cell phone. But you don't have money to help yourself get a job? When you don't get a job because of your appearance, you can use that cell phone to call your friends and family and ask them for money (until it gets shut off).

Clothing

Big network newscasters are the image of a professional individual. That is what you should be copying. Your individual style is for when you are off work, not for a job interview. Dressing in anything other than corporate attire will be a *distraction* and *prove* that you do not know how to dress appropriately for the work place.

Ladies and Gentelman may I have your attention? Please wear a navy-blue or black suit . Get your pants hemmed correctly. Invest in alterations to look good in that suit. It will pay off.

TRUE STORY #2

Once I met with a woman in the dead of winter. She arrived at my office wearing a white suit with a rainbow that spanned from one sleeve around her back to the other sleeve. I didn't mention it until the end. Finally I said, "I would go with a blue or black suit."

She replied, "Well this suit makes me cheery."

"Does unemployment make you cheery?" is what I wanted to say...but didn't.

I kept explaining that she had to look professional for the office environment. She said she understood and promised not to wear that suit and follow my advice.

I sent her out on an interview and learned the hard way about defining the color blue. Turquoise blue was not what I meant. My ears got red when the client called and said "Jill what was this women wearing when you met her?"

My first thought was that she had on the rainbow suit again and she had lied to me. But I just tried to skate by and said, "Why, what did she have on?"

She told me a loud turquoise suit with white shoes and that she looked ridiculous. Lesson learned: not everyone will "get it." If someone is told what corporate attire is and they do not adhere to advice on how to achieve that look, they *prove* that they are going to ultimately do their own thing.

For the guys: attire
Guys, please wear an undershirt underneath your dress shirt, a short-sleeved white cotton undershirt. Not wearing an undershirt or one with no sleeves (i.e., the "wife-beater") under your pressed collared button-down dress shirt is not the best look. Corporate attire includes an undershirt under a dress shirt.

For both: no wrinkles
A wrinkle should not be found anywhere on your clothes on interview day. Press your suit *and* the shirt you are going to wear underneath. Better yet, pay the fee to have the dry cleaner's professionally press it. Let me say it one more time:

A WRINKLE SHOULD NOT BE FOUND ANYWHERE ON YOUR CLOTHES ON INTERVIEW DAY!

For both: Earrings, Piercings and Other Jewelry
A quick tip about earrings: Ready? Here we go: THEY ARE TO BE WORN BY WOMEN. In their lower ear lobes. Guys, take the Diddy-double diamonds out of your ears unless you are interviewing with him or another hip-hop mogul. In all honesty guys: wear a watch and a wedding band if you are married. That's it.

If you have a piercing in your nose, eyebrow, upper ear lobe, tongue: take it out. Even to meet a recruiter.

No large, loud jewelry i.e.: big-hoop earrings, lots of gold bracelets, or necklaces that are over-bearing with lots of colors or jewels in them. Small pearl earnings and a thin pearl necklace works best. A tasteful necklace or stud earrings are okay as well.

Ties
Guys: wear a tie, but not a loud one. What kind of tie is Anderson Cooper wearing? I bet it is does not have a red queen of hearts in the middle of it. Don't have the money to buy a tie? Find it: ask for it, earn it, or borrow it. You found the money to go to Subway and a movie; you don't need that much for a new tie! It is a worthwhile investment: it's worth more than a night out? Ya think?

If you don't know how, learn to tie a tie. If the knot is too small it looks ridiculous. If the tie is too short or too long it looks ridiculous. You need to look perfectly professional. Go to any men's store and ask the salesman which knot is currently in fashion and how to tie it.

Hairstyle
Ladies
Pay attention to what your hair says about you. If you have kinky curly hair, get a blow out at the salon for the interview. I highly recommend it. You will look sleek and more stylish. If your hair is straight keep it combed, clean, and neat, and never in your face or sprayed up in the air with hairspray. If it is long, that's fine, just keep it back and professional looking. If you color your hair and you picked a color that doesn't look natural, get it colored again to look like human hair. It's simple: *If you arrive at the interview with burgundy hair you will not get the job.*

> ***TRUE STORY #3***
> Someone came in to meet with me a short time ago. Her hair was in a tall bun on the very top of her head. She was trying to look professional. She had on a beautiful suit and seemed professional. My advice to her right off the bat was to change her hair style. She didn't want to. OK, fine. I tried again later on the interview. Maybe just pin your hair back with a bun in back of her head. Nope: she didn't like that option either. We finished the interview politely and when she left I put her paperwork in my file drawer and did not refer her to any of my clients.

Why? I wasn't sending her to my client looking like Marge Simpson. Her hairstyle would have caused the client to focus on that and not on her. When she left, the client would have called me and asked me "Jill, what were you thinking sending her to me with that hair style? That doesn't work here, you know that." OK, now I am not saying she will never get a job. She may...but it will take longer. I assure you: if a recruiter makes a suggestion, go with it.

Gentlemen
Clean cut—that's right—cut your hair. Long and shaggy is a great look for nights and weekends, but your cool hairstyle is not going to help you get a job. Let your appearance go into a professional's hands. Go to a good barber or salon and tell them, "I am going to look for a job. Please cut my hair to look professional."

If you have been getting the same crew cut for 15 years, try letting it grow in a little bit. Have the barber use a number 3 or 4 blade instead of the 1 or 2. Short, nicely groomed hair is best (like a newscaster). If you are balding and shave your head totally, fine. But do not shave lines in it. If the barber suggested trimming your eyebrows, say "Yes!" Nose and ear hair don't work, either.

Facial Hair
Ladies
Thing is—if you have a hairy upper lip—I believe that you know it. But here's how to be sure. If you can stand in the bathroom and look in the mirror under normal lighting and see it on your face, everyone else can see it too. Sorry, but women should not have mustaches. So wax it because it is not doing you any favors. In any nail salon, lip waxing is available for $5 to $10. Invest and look better. It's painful you say? Please. Pain is hearing someone say "You look like a man."

Gentlemen
Clean-shaven is ideal. You cannot go wrong with a smooth face. Again, think about it: How many news anchors besides Geraldo sport a mustache or beard or goatee? If you insist, understand the risk. At least make damn sure that it is trimmed appropriately. No strange shaving patterns on your face. That is distracting and not professional.

Briefcases and Handbags
Arrive carrying **one** bag, a professional briefcase. It should match the color of your shoes (and belt if you are wearing one.) Inside should be a folder with at least **five** copies of your resume. (You never know how many people you might be meeting that day; it would be nice to have a copy for everyone). Also carry a list of your references and their **current** phone numbers.
You may have to write those references and phone numbers on the application given to you when you arrive at the company. Be prepared. One last thing: carry a clean pad of paper to jot down notes as the interviewer is speaking. This will be noticed and means points for you! (Bring your own pen.)

Shoes
Make sure they are comfortable. Guys: Make sure they are shined. Ladies: If you are wearing high heels to the interview *do not* carry them in a little plastic bag and then change from your sneakers to your heels in the lobby. Always show up interview-ready.

Do not wear high heels that hurt your feet and make you have to take them off in the lobby and wince when you put them back on.

Socks and Stockings
Every last detail counts here, people. You went and got the suit and it fits perfectly and you forget to buy new black socks or a new pair of stockings. Ahh! Don't forget. You cannot achieve a polished look without the complete accessories. Baggy old blue socks don't go with your suit. White socks also don't go with a suit. When you sit down they *will* be noticed and you will look odd and unprepared. Same thing with stockings, so ladies make sure yours do not have runs in them if you are wearing a skirt. Get a new pair before you go to an interview so you know they are in good shape. Baggy stockings with runs or holes look terrible. *Pay attention to detail in your clothes and that* proves *you will pay attention to detail in your work.*

Speaking of skirts—ladies—nothing too short. You look low-class no matter how thin and great your legs are. We are not in a bar. And wear plain sheer panty hose or stockings, never fish-net stockings or anything with designs on them or bold colors. You are in an office, not a club. (You know who you are.)

Cell phones
TURN THEM **OFF** *BEFORE* YOU ENTER THE BUILDING! Enough said.

Body Weight
In my experience I have found that weight can hold people back from fulfilling their potential. Don't let that happen to you. Few of us are the perfect size, and most people could afford to lose a few pounds. But, what I mean is: Don't look sloppy. If you look sloppy in every suit and formal outfit you try on you should lose enough weight to look professional. There are stores for all shapes and sizes. So look polished! This will help during interviews with how you feel and how you look. Also wear the appropriate size clothing. Some people are heavier but it doesn't matter because they are neat and polished in spite of their extra pounds. Being neat and polished can happen at almost any size. But if you find that your weight is interfering in your presentation then lose weight.

Save the Ta-Tas
I know you love your ta-tas, your hoo-hahs, your boobies, your breasts—whatever it is you call them. We all love them, BUT... *Please* leave them out of the interview

process. If they are small we don't need to see them peeping out of your shirt like darts. Wear a padded bra, thank you. If they are large they'd better not be pouring out of your shirt. They will be distracting to the interviewer. During the interview we have to make believe we are not noticing them. So put them away please. Thanks. You don't have to hide them completely; just wear the proper clothes. Nothing too tight or too low cut. Don't show cleavage. It is unprofessional.

Make Up & Nails

Question: Do you think Katie Couric's lipstick color is called "Juicy Delicious"? It's not. If you don't know how to tone it down go to the counter at a department store and tell the women at the counter you are going out on a job interview and allow her to do your make-up for you. It will cost you nothing (unless you buy products) and you will learn about day tones and evening tones. You should wear some make-up but not too much.

Keep nails short with light shades of polish, this is much more chic than red talons. Long nails also won't help your typing score.

Do You Smoke?

Don't smoke before your interview and go in there stinking like smoke. Never a good idea because most people do not smoke and it turns them off if you smell like an ashtray.

Tattoos

Do not show them anywhere at any time on your body. If you have tattoos hide them as best you can. They are not helping your cause. They might help you get a date or express yourself but again this is not about you, remember? So cover them up: they are a distraction. If you don't have tattoos, great.

Here is a few words to the wise: **Don't ever** get a tattoo anywhere that will show in a short sleeve shirt or (for women) skirts. And if you have a tattoo on your hands or neck (or anywhere they are visible if dressed in a suit) I would advise getting them professionally removed. That's right. Are you shocked? Don't be! Tattoos are still unprofessional for mostly every working environment, even if Brad and Angelina have them.

Body Odor And Perfume

If you have body odor because you don't bathe often, you know it. Come on! That is what we (who don't smell) are thinking. We think you know and you don't care, because how could you not know? Again, here is a way for you to figure it out for sure. If you do not shower at *least* every three days and use deodorant *every day* you probably have body odor. Take care of yourself. If you look good and smell great you will feel better. Newsflash: You should shower and use deodorant every day you go into work. This is the 21st century after all.

And let me tell you right now if you wear too much colon or perfume you will not get the job and I promise you that. Other people cannot stand when someone's heavy perfume comes into the room with them. It gives people a headache. So if you spray all over *everyday*, and all your clothes smell like that same perfume or cologne, knock it off.

One other thing: MAKE SURE YOU HAVE FRESH BREATH GOING INTO AN INTERVIEW. Bad breath = no offer. Mints will work, but gum-chewing is another BIG FAT NO.

What Language Was That? Those Regional And Ethnic Accents Are Not Gaining You Any Points.

I was born and raised on Long Island. My parents grew up in Brooklyn. I know that I have an accent and I have always done my very best to speak correctly when dealing with anyone at work. I made sure of it because I listened to others and to myself and knew that my accent was not acceptable for the work place. I figured this out very quickly. There are plenty of people I meet that are into their 40s and still have no idea of how unprofessional they sound. You must not only look like those newscasters, but also try to mimic the way they talk. If you have an accent, by now you should know. You are a grown up. Beware of accents. They are not professional. Use the English language correctly. For some odd reason this does not include those with British or Australian accents. Why? I don't know. Americans love those accents and in a professional setting they are welcome. My young son was recently at a dinner table with two friends from England. He whispered to me "Mommy, they are rich, right?"

Extreme regional accents and slang are a distraction and they *prove* you are not able to use the English language correctly. A slight accent is fine; we all have certain words that give away where we were raised. But saying, "I axed you" instead of "I asked you" and not being aware of how you sound is not acceptable. If you are not sure of the difference between a slight regional accent and an extreme one, get a tape recorder and tape your speaking voice. Turn on ABC, NBC, or CBS, and listen to the news. Then listen to yourself again. If you sound like you are speaking a different language than they are, you'd better fix it.

> ***TRUE STORY #4***
> Last year I met Lisa. She was applying for a job as an executive assistant for a Hedge Fund. She had every last qualification for the job: Amazing typing skills of 88 words per minute, PowerPoint, Excel, MS Word. She was beautiful and poised. She was dressed lovely. She was kind and had a pleasant way about her. I thought she was terrific. But, born and raised in Staten Island, she had a strong accent. During the interview, I arranged an appointment for her with an elite company that was looking for a secretary with her exact type of experience. I explained what to do and what not to do on the job interview; she listened to me for a long time. I explained to her everything she would need to know to ace the interview. And mentioned her accent in a nice way. She nodded her head the entire time. (I thought—surprise!—she took it well what I said about her accent) Finally, she said to me, "Jill, ok I got all dat. But, let me axe you one more ding."
>
> She didn't get hired. She didn't even get a second interview. Take a guess why. Well, it was a few *dings*. What I said went right over her head. I learned this: If you are 45 years old and you don't know you have an accent, you'll never know to listen for it. Lisa did get a job but it took her seven months! And whenever I sent her out I said "She has a heavy accent. Is that okay?" This way my client was forewarned. And to be honest, a few times clients said "No, I don't want to see her. That won't work here."

The Don't List

- Don't say:
  - ✓ the word *like* a million times while you are talking (You will sound *like* a 13-year-old girl.)
  - ✓ *yep* or *yeah*. Say YES.
  - ✓ *nope* or *nah*. Say NO.
  - ✓ *okay*, *right*, *you know*, or *you know what I mean?* Don't say those phrases!
  - ✓ *axe* instead of ASK
  - ✓ Word *perfick*. The word is PERFECT
  - ✓ *ain't?* Try "ISN'T" or better yet, "IS NOT"
  - ✓ *ya'll* and/or *all-ya'll*
  - ✓ *ah-right* instead of ALRIGHT
  - ✓ *ig-nert* instead of IGNORANT (Drives me nuts!)
  - ✓ *Kinney-garden* instead ofKINDERGARTEN
  - ✓ *Brek-fiss* instead of BREAKFAST
  - ✓ *Pitcher* instead of PICTURE
  - ✓ *Drug "attic"* instead of ADDICT
  - ✓ *Win-diz* instead of WIDOWS
- Don't use slang expressions or any type of language that is unprofessional—no matter how comfortable you feel with the interviewer.
  - ✓ *Bro', Man, Dude, Guy, Bud, Champ, etc.*
  - ✓ *How you feelin'?* or *How you do'en?* or *Good to meet ch'a.* These are *not* good openers!
  - ✓ *Have a good one*—not a way to say goodbye
  - ✓ *Be good*—again, not a way to say goodbye
- Don't EVER curse on an interview. Even if the interviewer is cursing up a storm, do not use foul language of any kind. It is uncalled for and low-class.

Improve Your "On-Line" APPEARANCE
WebPages, websites, and blogs

Guess what? That's right! More and more everyday companies are checking the Web to see what type of attitude, behavior, and character people *really* have. BE CAREFUL what you post online. If they are on the fence about hiring you, potential employers might just check to see what you have on your web page. It just might cost you the job you don't have yet. **SO CLEAN IT UP!** Take out those Spring Break pictures. It can ruin your career and you will never even know how or when or why.

What Are You Thinking Right Now?

After reading all of this, you might be saying, "This is who I AM". Yes...that is nice. Then perhaps you can get a job in a tattoo parlor. Maybe Kat Van D will hire you. But seriously, if you are reading this and feel you must change too much for corporate America, you should try getting a job where you can be yourself completely. Try to find a place or business that match your own guidelines on appearance. But know that even in the most laid-back companies, people need to look professional on an interview. If you don't, you will probably not get the job.

Another thing is that employees often work with as a team. You will need to be on the same page as the others in the office. If someone says: "No, this is who I am," that means they are not flexible and won't be good at fitting in with a team. Not everyone in any office looks alike. There are people with nose rings in an office. There are people with tattoos. There are people that wear buns on top of their heads. But they didn't get hired with those things exposed on an interview. At least not at a corporation with a paid vacation plan, 401k and stock options.

This is not discrimination. This is not about race, gender, age, or religion. It is about personal appearance and what that *proves* about a person. If a company does not want to hire someone because of a nose ring, tattoo, or smiley face tie, *they won't*. But that job seeker won't be told the real reason why. They will be told they weren't qualified or over-qualified or whatever other excuse an employer wants to make up. Fortunately, now you know the truth.

My experience has shown that heeding all of this advice results in obtaining a position faster. **You cannot pick and choose which things to follow.** This is like a recipe. If you leave one thing out, it is not award-winning: it is mediocre. You need every ingredient to achieve the reward...the job offer.

Chapter Five

THE ABCs: ATTITUDE, BEHAVIOR, AND CHARACTER

This is the part that can make the community-college graduate get the job over the Ivy League graduate. You can put into effect everything in this book, but if your attitude stinks, your behavior is poor, and you show zero character, then you will not get hired. This is not a threat. It is a promise.

ATTITUDE

"The longer I live, the more I realize the impact of attitude on life. Attitude, to me, is more important than facts. It is more important than the past, than the education, than the money, than the circumstances, than failure, than successes, than what other people think or say or do. It is more important than appearance, giftedness, or skill. It will make or break a company...a church...a home. The remarkable thing is we have a choice everyday regarding the attitude we will embrace for that day. We cannot change our past and we cannot change the fact that people will act in a certain way. We cannot change the inevitable. The only thing we can do is to play on the one string we have, and that is our attitude. I am convinced that life is 10% what happens to me and 90% of how I react to it. And so it is with you: we are in charge of our attitudes."
-Charles Swindoll (pastor, author, educator, and radio personality)

Be likable and enjoyable to converse with. This is all about attitude. I don't care what your facial features are or what body type you have: when it comes to likability, those things are irrelevant. It doesn't matter what race or origin you are. If you are poor or rich or if you were treated badly by your parents, it you does not make any difference. *You have an ability to be likable no matter what.* Do not allow anyone to tell you otherwise.

People can have issues with their attitude whether their parents were terrific or horrible. Let's say you were praised all your life and your parents gave you the utmost attention, now you may need to realize that you are not in fact the center of the world. That is a difficult thing to realize. If you were raised entitled and if it affected your attitude, you are going to find yourself in trouble out there. Same thing applies if you were put down all your life and your self-esteem was stripped from you. You are now an adult and need to realize that you have worth and you can be a success. Get past your negative upbringing. You are an adult—it is finally in your hands.

"Happiness is an attitude. We either make ourselves miserable, or happy and strong. The amount of work is the same."
-Francesca Reigler (author, motivational speaker)

Also it doesn't matter what school you graduated from: depth and character cannot be taught at an Ivy League school, same as they cannot be taught at high school. So don't hide behind your school. Princeton, Harvard, or Yale graduates don't get all the jobs—so stop thinking that the golden path is smoothly paved for you just because you have your degree from a top university. Community college students: listen up! You are just as viable a candidate as anyone else, so don't knock yourself down. Have a humble attitude if you were fortunate enough to get a degree from Harvard. If you got your degree at Suffolk County Community College, have strength and optimism in your attitude, because the fact is, you worked hard and got it.

Attitude is what drives both your behavior and character. How behavior and character are presented and perceived will depend upon your attitude.

BEHAVIOR

"You can't talk your way out of what you behaved yourself into."

-Stephen R. Covey (author of *The Seven Habits of Highly Effective People*)

Your behavior *proves* who you are. Going in to an interview with tattoos exposed on your hands or neck and a nose ring is *proving* you do your own thing. Talking loudly on a cell phone in the waiting area *proves* you are rude. Not saying please and thank you to the receptionist because she is "nobody important" *proves* your lack of empathy. No matter what you say or how pleasant you seem to be, your behavior will be a dead giveaway that you will do what *you* feel like doing. You are not going to get started in any job *behaving* like that.

Ultimately a person's attitude is going to affect their behavior. If you have a negative attitude it *proves* you will behave that way. If you are in a bad mood on a certain day chances are you weren't on your best behavior. If I am in a bad mood then no one else matters but me. That is how I act when I am in a bad mood. I act selfishly.

In terms of interviewing others, certain behaviors can *prove* things about people. For example, poor eye contact or not looking at you in the eye when you are speaking to them *proves* they are hiding themselves. When someone can't look at me, it makes me wonder. Maybe they are lying. Maybe they are insecure. Maybe they are afraid. Maybe they were abused. Maybe they hate themselves. Maybe they hate others. In any event, I don't want to hire them. They can't show themselves, so they failed the interview no matter what they said or how good their resume looked. I don't like when people "laser eye" me either, staring right at me for the entire interview, like a timid deer in the headlights or a determined serial killer. Ugh! Labored eye contact is not good.

Also it is disconcerting when people stare at my mouth while I am speaking to them and not at my eyes or face. There must be a comfortable balance for the interviewer not to sense your uneasiness. If your behavior is too meek or too edgy, they will want to get you out of their office as quickly as possible.

Another example: People who constantly interrupt me while I am speaking. That is poor behavior and it *proves* their need for dominance. They want the control. Any type of bad manners *proves* selfishness. Not holding a door open for the person behind you, or not saying please or thank you. You should behave in a manner that *proves* you are considerate of others. Sending a hand-written thank-you note after an interview with a kind message *proves* you are truly appreciative that someone spent their time with you.

The strange thing is, it seems to happen naturally to the people who have a positive attitude. If you are happy with yourself and in a great mood, top-notch behavior seems to follow. You just attract people to you and you can't seem to help it. Same for a negative attitude, you lose job opportunities again and again and you can't seem to help it.

Be There

Be in the moment. That is one of the biggest issues with people today. Are you listening to someone else while they are speaking or are you just looking at them and thinking things about them to yourself? *You must be present.* I know when someone is interviewing with me and they are not really listening and not engaged. I want them out of my office as soon as possible. They are rude and it is all over them that they can not focus. NEXT!

CHARACTER
(AND HAVING "IT")

My good friend Annemarie married a guy whose nephew was born with Down Syndrome. His name is Thomas.

Whenever I get to see Thomas at family parties. I find it amazing how loving and affectionate he is towards those people he likes. He loves my husband to pieces. Although Thomas doesn't see him often, when we do get together, Thomas always gives my husband hugs throughout the day..."I love YOU, man", they say to each other. I commented to Annemarie about Thomas and she said: "Ya know Jill, if you ever want to know if someone is good, honest, or genuine, just introduce them to Thomas. See how Thomas reacts to them, and vice versa. If Thomas likes them, they are okay."

I wish I could bring Thomas into the conference room of my office when I interview applicants. He would surely help me separate the keepers from the phonies. Thomas has an ability to perceive an individual's character better than most of us. Often our judgment is clouded by money or looks or social status (either good or bad). Thomas does not have a clouded judgment; he could care less what someone looks like, whether they live in a mansion or on the street, or how popular they are. He is judging them based upon what he should be: how they make him feel. When Thomas is dealing with other people, there is no past or future; he is always in the present. He is real.

Having Downs Syndrome is simply one of Thomas' characteristics that make up who he is. Anyone who feels uncomfortable around him is the one with the disability. When faced with someone authentic like Thomas, those with a lack of character simply cannot deal with it. They try to hide. *We should be aware of others to the highest possible extent*. This is having good character.

"You can easily judge the character of a man by how he treats those who can do nothing for him."
-James D. Miles (Motivational Speaker)

Say hello to the security guard, the cleaning lady, and the doorman. Why? They are just like you...they are a human beings, living their life and doing their job. They like being noticed and welcomed just as you do.

Character is the totality of one's depth, charm, temperament, genuineness, personality, and disposition. A person's character is often what makes the difference on an interview. It is what will set apart two people with a similar skill set; or even propel a less qualified candidate to get hired. When asked, the interviewer simply says, "They just had **IT.**"

Ever hear someone say, "You either have **IT** or you don't"? Well, what *is* **IT**? And why is **IT** clearly demonstrated in someone's character? In my experience, having **IT is not only one's ability to relate to others but also a person's core**

belief in him- or herself. Or what I like to call someone's *success*. This success is not about being wealthy or famous, it is more intimate. Let me explain:

A while ago, I read an interview with famous designer Tom Ford in the magazine *Vanity Fair*. In it he said: *"I have been successful because I would never hire anyone I wouldn't go to dinner with."* Mr. Ford is one of the most successful designers and businessmen on the planet. I was so proud of myself when I read that because I have been saying the same thing about recruiting (but I say "lunch" instead of "dinner").

For years I have advised my staff: if you wouldn't go to lunch with an applicant, don't send them out to a client. Why? Who wants to go to lunch with someone who doesn't believe in him- or herself and who has no confidence? It's like work. I find it hard to connect with these people. They are not inferior to me, but they might act that way because they think they are. They may be shy and quiet or worse, they are constantly "selling" themselves in the conversation. Either way, it doesn't make for a good lunch partner nor does it make for a good employee. They don't believe themselves to be a success yet. These are the people who fail at interviews again and again. These people don't have **IT** because they just don't get it.

When you have **IT**, you own your success and a *quiet confidence* resides in you. This confidence has no bravado and requires no sales pitch. Have you ever met a Special Forces operator or a Navy Seal? I have interviewed them and they never hinted at their title. They simply said that they were in the Army or the Navy. I had to pry it out of them. Successful people never sell themselves. They simply *show* their success with their attitude, their behavior, and most importantly, their character.

So, what are companies ultimately looking for in an employee? Answer is, they want to hire people who own their success; people who have **IT**. Why? Because these people have character and realize that success is a daily process. It is ongoing.

To laugh often and much;
To win the respect of intelligent people and the affection of children;
To earn the appreciation of honest critics and endure the betrayal of false friends;
To appreciate beauty, to find the best in others;
To leave the world a bit better, whether by a healthy child, a garden patch or a redeemed social condition;
To know even one life has breathed easier because you have lived.
This is to have succeeded.
-Ralph Waldo Emerson

Again, success is intimate. It does not come with a degree or with someone saying, "You're hired." Many college graduates *believe* they are a success because of their degree, but they do not really own it. They earned a diploma from a good college or university; and now carry this "bravado" into interviews. They try to sell themselves and four months later they feel like a failure because they haven't landed a job. That is immature.

Those who recognize each day as an *opportunity to give of yourself*, to make an effort to be a useful part of your world (with your job, your child, or your garden) have character. These are the ones who know success. They have **IT**. They are a success, not because of a degree, but because of who they are—and they get the job!

ABCs And The Interview

The way to *prove* something on an interview is to *show* it, not to say it or "sell" it. You can explain yourself, talk about your life and your experiences, and describe what you've achieved. But was anything learned from these experiences and achievements? Or were you just going through the motions: completing a predetermined checklist for your resume? Either way, it will be *shown* in your ABCs. Your attitude, your behavior and your character will come across almost instantly on an interview. They will *prove* that either you get it or you don't.

How I Got It

IT came to me through being a waitress. I had other jobs in the past, but I did not take anything away from them except a paycheck. After my sophomore year of college, my parents stopped paying my tuition. Boy, was I mad when I found out my parents couldn't pay for the next two years of school. I cried and told them I hated them for "ruining my life." If I wanted to continue my education, I was going to have to become a waitress.

This was the first time in my life where I learned about sacrifice and hard work. I quickly realized that the more I busted my butt, the more money I made. I learned to love my job and balance it with school. Waitressing enabled me to pay my tuition and graduate from Hofstra University. I worked so hard with a smile and every shift was another chance to wait the perfect table, to get everything running smoothly and perfect my job. I was not perfect but I strived to be. It showed in my tips. I now owned a work ethic: this was my success. It gave me a quiet confidence because I now KNEW (from experience) that I could provide for myself.

That is why I was hired for *Live!* When they met me, they thought "Yeah, she's got **IT**! Hire her." I never had to say, "I am a success." All I had to say was "I will work my tail off." I had a quiet confidence because I was already a success and I *proved* it on the interview with my attitude, behavior and character. A job with them would only be another opportunity for me to continue my success.

ENHANCING YOUR ABCs

You cannot teach someone to have a great attitude, good behavior, or a strong character in one day. What I have noticed while interviewing several college graduates a week for the past 12 years is that this is the area of the hiring process where you can shine. Your generation has grown up with positive feedback. Many of you have traveled extensively and have an understanding of other cultures. You are well read. It is wonderful to meet people aged 22 to 29 and witness firsthand the future of America. However, because you are younger, the presentation of your ABCs will need fine-tuning. If you are not careful, you will be perceived by members of an older generation as "the E word": *Entitled*.

The trick here is to be conscious of how you show yourself to other people. With that awareness, your ABCs can be enhanced to make you more attractive on an interview. How do you do this? Well...there are a few ways, but I first want to focus on the easiest and most effective way of all: ***listening***.

Think for a moment about someone in your life that you truly admire. Someone that you set apart from all others...a professor, an uncle or cousin, a close friend, or maybe it's your mom or dad. Okay. Have them in your mind? Good. Now what is it that sets them apart?

THEY LISTEN TO YOU. When you speak to them, they are listening to what you are saying, digesting it, and speaking back to you about WHAT YOU SAID TO THEM. They are *involved in conversation* with *YOU*. It is not always about their thoughts, feelings and concerns and getting them into the conversation. They actually communicate WITH someone else. They have empathy. *And that ability to put yourself in someone else's shoes is the single most important way to enhance your ABCs*. Having the ability to listen when others speak, turning off the voice in your head, and paying full attention to another human being is GOLD.

It is the reason why some people connect with you on a higher level and some (most) don't. It is not that the people who don't really listen, don't care for you. Most do, but they are simply selfish. I am someone who for years never really listened to others while they spoke to me. I was hearing them, but my mind was occupied with my own personal agenda about the conversation. I got the "gist" of what they were saying early on and then shut off to focus my mind on my #1 thought...ME. I would focus my eyes on them, nod my head in agreement say "Yes,...that's right...sure...exactly," but I was not *even close* to listening to them and grasping what they were trying to convey. Then after "yes"ing them to death, I would have my chance to say what I was thinking about while they were speaking to me. And back and forth we would go. Do you do this? You have to first be aware of it in order to STOP.

When I interview people, I find myself separating those who were listening and those who were not. I can separate the "listeners" from the "talkers." That is what interviewers are subconsciously trying to do while they are interviewing you. People who listen better *prove that they pay attention and are easier to train, easier to be around, and easier to work with*.

With some people, I still don't always focus and listen and I can't help it. But I try everyday to be in the moment and LISTEN and put them first. I'll tell ya, for me...it is work (especially with my children). When you have a child, being a listener is NUMERO UNO. If a parent, for the entire course of a child's young life does not LISTEN, the child will eventually stop trying to talk to their mom or dad. Their parents don't listen anyway, so why keep trying? Even a four-year-old knows when someone is *"yes"ing* them and not really listening.

When it is necessary, parents *want* to listen to a sixteen-year-old to figure out what is going on in their life, but by then it is too late. You have to start young. But it is not easy. Most often, parents try to give it *all* to their children but work and schedules make it hard to listen. If your parents weren't really listening to you, YOU probably don't listen either. Realize it now and stop the cycle!

How Do Interviewers Know If You Are Really Listening or Not?

Your response will give you away. You must converse with them in a thoughtful give-and-take. Do not interject your thought process when responding during the interview. Interjecting what *you need for them to know about you,* makes it all about you. But this is *your interview* and you have to get it all in there, right? WRONG. This interview is about *the job* and if you can do it. Respond to questions and comments and *show* good ABCs. When you SELL YOURSELF you are simply setting up time to be a "talker" on the interview. You have the agenda. That does not work! Your responses must be about the interviewer's agenda.

Somehow, someway, put their comment or question back into your response. That will help.

Here are a few other ways to enhance your ABCs. Read on...

Reading Books

"The man who does not read books has no advantage over the man that cannot read them."
-Mark Twain

"The best of a book is not the thought which it contains, but the thought which it suggests; just as the charm of music dwells not in the tones but in the echoes of our hearts."
-Oliver Wendell Holmes

"I cannot live without books."
-Thomas Jefferson

"All good books are alike in that they are truer than if they had really happened and after you are finished reading one you will feel that all that happened to you and afterwards it all belongs to you; the good and the bad, the ecstasy, the remorse, and sorrow, the people and the places and how the weather was."
Ernest Hemingway

Put down *Star Weekly, Sports Illustrated*, and *People*. Stop logging onto the net every free minute to see the latest on You Tube. Pick up a good book. A classic, a NY Times bestseller, a biography, or the top business book: it doesn't matter. When we picked up our cliff notes, skimmed through them, and then wrote the 10-page paper the day before it was due, we lost something. We need to get it back now.

Reading a classic novel not only allows one to experience the human condition, but it teaches us to "read between the lines" of life and those around us.

Whenever we encounter a new character from a good novel, we now know that type of person. We will see them again in our life: we will meet people like that character. And when we do, the novel has already given us an insight into that person's mind. The more we read, the more characters we meet, and the sharper our instincts become. We had better understand an individual's motivations and ultimately their ABCs.

Whoa! Lighten up, you say. Okay, okay, you don't have to get that deep. Not a fan of classic novels? Any book that advances your knowledge on a personal area of interest will do. When I graduated college, I started to talk less and listen more. I learned that I didn't really know much about anything. So I began to read more. I read anything that interested me or that I wanted to know more about. It made a difference. I found myself able to speak more intelligently and actually contribute to a conversation. In the end, reading is the best alternative (and, alternatively, the best complement!) to experience: it is the research of life.

Question from Nicolas Varchaver to Warren Buffet: *"How do you get your ideas?"* His answer: *"I just read. I read all day."*
Fortune Magazine Interview, April 2008

Travel
"Traveling is a brutality. It forces you to trust strangers and to lose sight of all that familiar comfort of home and friends. You are constantly off balance. Nothing is yours except the essential things—air, sleep, dreams, the sea, the sky—all things tending towards the eternal or what we imagine of it."
-Cesare Pavese (Italian poet, novelist, literary critic)

"Travel is more than the seeing of sights; it is a change that goes on, deep and permanent, in the ideas of living."
-Miriam Beard (author of "A History of the Business Man")

"Travel is fatal to prejudice, bigotry, and narrow-mindedness."
-Mark Twain

Travel every chance you get. Even if you can only venture to the towns or cities around yours, go. Go to a strange place where you have never been and be enriched. Experience different cultures; it will challenge your own belief system. You will feel vulnerable and yet free from the constraints of your daily life.

Ever notice how the strong characters in a novel are the ones who travel? They are the characters we are most times supposed to learn a lesson from. Each time we travel somewhere new we have just broadened our horizons. It creates depth in a person so quickly is it amazing.

The Arts
"The holy grail is to spend less time making the picture than it takes people to look at it."
-Banksy (British Artist)

"You can't possibly hear the last movement of Beethoven's Seventh and go slow."
-Oscar Levant (composer, actor, and pianist, explaining his way out of a speeding ticket)

"Dancing is the loftiest, the most moving, the most beautiful of the arts. For it is no mere translation or abstraction of life. It is life itself."
-Henry Havelock Ellis (physician and social reformer)

"This music changed the shape of the room. It changed the shape of the world outside the room; the way you looked out the window and what you were looking at."
-Bono (Lead Singer / Song Writer - U2 on listening to John Lennon)

"A guy walks up to me and asks, 'What's Punk?' So I kick over a garbage can and say, 'That's punk!' So he kicks over a garbage can and asks, 'That's Punk?' and I say back, 'No, that's trendy!'"
-Billie Joe Armstrong (Musician)

"Imagine a world without photography, one could only imagine."
-Berenice Abbott (Photographer, Artist)

"We had gay burglars the other night. They broke in and rearranged the furniture."
-**Robin Williams (Actor/Comedian)**

"You are such a child, my dear. You think by saying 'I'm sorry' all the past can be forgiven."
-**Rhett Butler (Gone With the Wind)**

Go to a museum, an opera, a ballet, or a play. Enjoy a comedy show, a movie, or a rock concert. Or simply go outside and snap photographs. *Anything* that you can watch or listen to or be a part of; anything that you can immerse yourself in: these things will add to your character. It is an experience. If it makes you laugh or cry or wonder or wince, it is a good thing. A movie would work, especially if it's been nominated for an Oscar award. My point is for you to feel. Whether it comes from a painting or a soprano's solo or a guitar solo or a good belly laugh from a comedy club. Feel something by way of the Arts every day. Enrich your life with realty of the experience rather than merely with the TV remote.

Life...online
If you are on your computer all day long, texting, emailing, looking on *Facebook*, *MySpace, Twitter*, and sites that keep you informed of your life and others in it, let me tell you something: you are losing time with others and gaining isolation. This will eventually create odd behavior. You will lose interpersonal skills and you become aloof and difficult to talk with. You have to beware of not communicating with others face-to-face, or even by phone, on a daily basis. It is not healthy for your mind or your body to be on the computer constantly.

Do not allow yourself to become isolated. It is the wrong road to travel down. And most times it gets difficult to turn back once you go down that road and months turn into years. You won't know what to do to get back into the swing of things with other people. And when you do sit face-to-face with someone, it is terribly awkward. When I meet young people like this, it honestly makes me sad. They want so much to talk and be friendly, but they can't. They are smart and speak eloquently, but they cannot look at me or smile or sit confidently. They are disconnected. They always look as if they have not seen the light of day and are not energized. They speak in a monotone voice and they seem...off. And it is a shame: they know the computer inside and out, they score 100s on all the tests, they type fast, so much knowledge is inside them, but they won't be able to get a job that interacts with others. If someone does hire them, they will do so for a "computer research or data entry" type job. I hear recruiters say this all the time to their clients, *"Oh yeah. He is a real tech guy—has no problem sitting at a computer all day—he'd be perfect for your data-entry job."* Then this "tech guy" gets that job and is on the computer all day and all night. *Nice life huh?*

"A new young analyst started in my office, from the newest generation of highly educated professionals prepared for the particular position, however lacking interpersonal skills (and work experience). Equidistant from myself, the new employee and our secretary sat. The secretary received an email from this new employee asking for office supplies. Our secretary turned around to see the new employee sitting directly behind her at her work-station and was completely puzzled with the request. Instead of responding via email the secretary blurted out..."I'm sitting right here, come over and ask me what you need!" You definitely want excellent interpersonal skills and to have your secretary on your side so it's important to establish that relationship from the onset. Take a break from the computer and don't forget about water-cooler talk to start your reputation on the right foot."
-**Colleen S. (Government Intelligence Analyst)**

Continuing Education Thoughout Your Life
College should not be the end of your education. It should be the beginning. After so many years of education, I could not wait to finish college. But now, if I could sit in a classroom and have someone teach me something new, I would be in heaven. Why? I truly miss school. When I graduated college, that is the last thing I thought I would ever say. I was so sick of school, but you may find yourselves feeling the same way I do sooner than you think. Education is truly a key to life. It opens doors. The notion that college is the end is the biggest untruth we tell ourselves. You may not know it, but college has only prepared you for a lifetime of seeking out knowledge. Your teachers have wired you to want to learn (that is, if they did their jobs correctly) and there is no turning back. So take a class here and there on anything that interests you. It could be at a local community college or a workshop or a church. Sitting down with a group of people to learn is a glorious thing. You will probably not appreciate it until it is no longer a part of your life. And when you do go back you will have a lot more fun this time! I promise!

"Grace is to the body, what good manners are to the mind."

François de la Rochefoucauld
(French classical author)

Don't forget Please and Thank You
Good manners are the behaviors that will *prove* you to be considerate and mindful. They are extremely important and will have a huge impact (positive, if manners are used, or negative if they are not) on your interview.

Say to the interviewer upon arrival:
"It is a pleasure to meet with you today. Thank you for seeing me."
That is good manners. That is a way to say HELLO politely.

The wrong way is:
"Hey, how ya doing. Good to meetcha. I was waiting a while in reception but that is okay."
Or the plain ol' *"Hi."* When I meet someone and they only say "*Hi*", all I can think is "Please! Grow up!"
Or asking the interviewer: "How are you?"
You do not know them so don't ask that. It can be an awkward way to begin a conversation on an interview.

Use your manners with every single person you encounter on an interview. Don't overdo it; just be polite. When you exhibit good manners with kindness in your voice, you don't have to "sell" yourself on being good with customers. That is now obvious: you just *proved* that you are good with customers. It is that easy.

Unless the person meeting you tells you to call them by their first name, call them Mr. or Ms. or Miss or Mrs. and their last name, pronounced correctly. Call the receptionist or their secretary ahead of time and ask what they like to be called. They will tell you and be impressed you cared enough to call. When you arrive at the interview say "Thank you" to that person for the information. That is good manners. You may have just impressed the receptionist or secretary without doing much, just by having good manners.

I don't care if you are going to a Taco Bell for an interview; you call the interviewer Mr. or Ms., unless told otherwise. Even if they are younger than you; even if they are not dressed well, polished, or professional, even if they speak with a heavy accent and have stains on their clothes.

Why? Because they should be respected: someone has put THEM in charge of meeting with new hires. If you do not agree or at least understand why you should have some respect for the interviewer, put down this book and pick up the OTB (Off Track Betting) lists and try to make your money there. Good luck to you.

Experience And Work Ethic

"A dream doesn't become reality through magic; it takes sweat, determination, and hard work."

-Colin Powell (Retired General and former Secretary of State)

One of the most important things that can be *proven* by your ABCs is your work ethic. This will be molded from experiencing and excelling at a difficult job that makes you work until you are physically and/or mentally exhausted. Achieving a bachelor's degree, while balancing extracurricular activities can help create a good work ethic. Although it is just the beginning, it is credible. That is why more and more companies are requiring a degree. But make no mistake, a degree does not compensate for experience and it never will. If you put them together you are off to a great start.

The only thing school requires you to *know*, is "how to learn". Sick of hearing that one, I know, but it applies. Professors require you to recall things and create things, but they do not require you to gain experience. Attending college and learning about an industry means that you will be able to do the research and conclude how to solve a problem. It does not mean that you *know* what to do on the job, but only that you *can learn* what to do. Experience needs to come into play to *know* anything for certain.

You get it? This is why prior job experience is important for any college grad. Any job experience at all...part-time, full-time, anything. If you have this experience, guess what? You have demonstrated that you *know* how to hold down a job. I don't care if you worked at the Piggly Wiggly; you still experienced working every day. You were tired when you came home, but even on the days you hated it, you went back. This knowledge of work experience will be *proven* on the interview, because it is real. No one can take it away from you or contest that you did work and got paid for it. It will show in your ABCs.

Mistakes

Think of your first few visits home if you went away to college. Did you run into friends who were still in high school? Maybe you had the experience many of us do: they seemed young, possibly immature, and even sometimes clueless. They thought they knew all about college, but you had the experience and really knew. It is not one big party. Yet a year previous, you were the senior in high school and you thought you knew it all.

That is the same thing that is happening on job interviews. Many college graduates are interviewing as if they *know*, but to those who have experience and do *know*, we immediately get turned off. It is a sign of immaturity. BE CONSCIOUS OF WHAT YOU ACTUALLY KNOW, AND WHAT YOU ARE PROVING ABOUT YOURSELF.

> A young gentleman whom I placed in an entry-level job at a prestigious global law firm called me one day and said, "I do not want to get the attorneys coffee and that is what I was asked to do last week. I have a degree from an Ivy League college and they asked me for coffee. I want to *think* at my job; I want to use my mind to help them on the case. I did what they asked of me, I always do, but I am pissed off. This is not the job I signed up for."
>
> My response to him was: "Why would an attorney hire you to think for him? You know nothing about his case or any case for that matter." He was let go a few weeks after this conversation from one of the largest world-wide law firms on the planet. He let his ego get in the way and it stopped his opportunity.

Although he did what was asked of him, his ABCs proved something else about him. His ABCs got him fired. In this case, getting coffee allows YOU to be the one that *knows* how the attorneys like their coffee. NOW YOU *KNOW*. Now they don't need to hire someone to get them coffee. That is now your experience. Do it the best you can because if you can get their coffee right, hang around and next time you can get the court documents ready and run them to court. Then you will *know* where the downtown courthouse is, instead of THINKING YOU *KNOW*. Are you starting to *get it*?

Evaluate Yourself

- What are your experiences?
- What do you *know* as opposed to what you *think* you know?
- Have your experiences effected your ABCs ?
- Do you have **IT**? In what areas of your life do you own your success? In which skills and talents does *your* quiet confidence reside?

Chin Up

You have to start somewhere. Below is a list of where some of the most successful and most ordinary people started their jobs. Rest assured nothing is beneath you.

Michael Dell, founder and chairman of Dell Computer Corp. was a dishwasher at a Chinese restaurant earning $2.30 an hour when he was young.

Bill Gates, founder of Microsoft, was a congressional page at the Washington state Capitol.

William Watkins, current CEO of Seagate Technology, worked the night shift at a mental hospital restraining people who got out of control.

Rush Limbaugh shined shoes.

Tommy Hilfiger originally sold his jeans from the trunk of his car when no one would hire him and he had no money to get a store.

Warren Buffet worked in his grandfather's grocery store for years.

Best selling author Stephen King was a school Janitor.

Ted Turner rebuilt his father's bankrupt company from the ground up. He had nothing and was in debt when his father died.

George Steinbrenner sold eggs from the family chicken farm to his rural Ohio neighbors for years while he went to school.

Oprah Winfrey at 16 was an on-air reporter earning $100 per week.

Colin Powel swept floors in a warehouse while in college.

Ask the people in your life (parents, aunts, uncles, teachers, neighbors, grandparents) where they started working when they were young. Ask them the hours they worked and how much money they made. We are not royalty. We are all regular people, just like everyone else, and so are you. And you have to pay dues just like everyone else.

Ironically, when they tell you about those hard times I bet most of them will smile. They remember it fondly. Why? Because of the simplest reason of all: they were young. You are young, so do the work that goes along with it. You will probably never look or feel as good as you do now. And I can assure you that you will not have this much energy.

Chapter Six

ACE THE INTERVIEW

They called or emailed. They would like to meet with you. YOU HAVE AN INTERVIEW!

The most important thing you can do in preparation for an interview (and in life for that matter) is to develop an *awareness* of how you are perceived by others. What cultural or societal stereotypes exist that you could be subjected to, either before an interview or upon first meetings? How are you perceived? This knowledge and awareness will enable you to temper your personality and tailor it to the job.

The Generational Disconnect and The New Stereotype Around Town
In today's job market there exists a "disconnect" between recent college graduates of the "millennial generation" who need a job and those of the generations before you that do the hiring. You think that they should hire you because you are YOU; and *they* think you were handed everything in life and don't know how to work for it. Fortunately, since I communicate with both sides I can get you to understand each other.

To understand *their* side, *you* must recognize the fact that many of the kids from your generation were raised with constant praise, instant gratification and the importance of self-confidence; all of which has produced in them a sense of *entitlement*. Their expectations are high and their work ethic is often too low. It is usually caused from unrealistic expectations fed to them by their parents combined with too much praise. During the interview they try to "sell" their individuality and do not understand that employers simply want a competent and hard worker. Ask yourself: Is this you?

Are you Entitled? What They Are Saying About You and Why...
"Have you noticed the growing trend of children and teens who believe the world owes them something? They feel entitled to the good life...preferably without any effort on their part. The recipe that leads to this self-centered attitude in children usually contains a guilt-ridden parent or two and a child who watches an average of 40,000 slick commercials each year. The children want; the parents give; the parents feel less guilty.

Here is one common scenario: Many parents, especially mothers, feel guilty for working long hours away from home. Some try to make it up to their children by doing and buying more and expecting less from them. Before long, they become indulgent, permissive parents; they cannot say "no" to their children. The children become self-centered and demanding. The term "spoiled brat" comes to mind. Permissive parenting seldom has a positive outcome for children.
-Tom McMahon (Parenting Expert)

Uh-Oh. Is this guy right? This disconnect is a growing issue in the American workplace. You should know this is a common *stereotype* of your generation. Going into an interview, it is a trait that most prospective employers will assume you possess. You will have to overcome this prejudice and *prove* yourself to be different with your ABCs.

How Are You Perceived?
Preparation for the interview also entails gaining an *honest* understanding of who you are. To be successful in any interview you must have an awareness of how you

are perceived. Many employers through the years have told me the same thing: "I know if I am going to hire someone within fifteen minutes talking with them." Why? How can an interviewer say that? Answer: It is how that person is perceived. It is their ABCs at work for or against them.

How will others perceive you from your resume? How does it define you? How are you perceived when others meet you for the first time? Perception of oneself is a difficult thing to recognize. It is very easy for us to know how we feel about others and what vibe they give off. But we really never know how others perceive us.

The following exercise is something that can help you understand how others perceive you. Read the poem below and try to identify how you were raised. It is easier to agree that you grew up with something than it is to see what you are now. It is easier for some people to say, "Yes, I grew up with criticism every day of my young life" than it is for them to admit that they condemn others. It will show both the positive and negative in your personality and give you a window into how you are perceived.

Children Learn What They Live
By Dorothy Law Nolte, Ph.D.
If children live with criticism, they learn to condemn.
If children live with hostility, they learn to fight.
If children live with fear, they learn to be apprehensive.
If children live with pity, they learn to feel sorry for themselves.
If children live with ridicule, they learn to feel shy.
If children live with jealousy, they learn to feel envy.
If children live with shame, they learn to feel guilty.
If children live with encouragement, they learn confidence.
If children live with tolerance, they learn patience.
If children live with praise, they learn appreciation.
If children live with acceptance, they learn to love.
If children live with approval, they learn to like themselves.
If children live with recognition, they learn it is good to have a goal.
If children live with sharing, they learn generosity.
If children live with honesty, they learn truthfulness.
If children live with fairness, they learn justice.
If children live with kindness and consideration, they learn respect.
If children live with security, they learn to have faith in themselves and in those about them.
If children live with friendliness, they learn the world is a nice place in which to live.

If you lived with kindness and consideration you probably *do* respect others. If you grew up with hostility you probably are quick to fight. If you notice the bad stuff you will be more likely to alter your behavior but you have to realize it first. Just don't go back and blame your parents. (They grew up with the same stuff.)

You are now responsible for changing yourself because *now you know*. You are an adult and you have the experience of living and living with others. We all know what right and wrong is. Right makes you feel good and wrong makes you feel bad. You are responsible now for your fate and how you are perceived.

Let me add four more of my own:
If children live with responsibility, they learn liability.
If children live with limits, they learn discipline.

If children live without modesty, they learn to be pompous.
If children live with instant gratification, they expect everything for nothing.

So put yourself into these sentences and write down what you grew up with. Chances are it will be a window to how others see you. Ask your friends for help on this. It is the *childhood friends* who can help out the best here.

Do not ask your parents to explain how others perceive you. Asking a parent is as good (or bad) as asking yourself. Siblings aren't much help either. They probably know your authenticity better than anyone (including your parents) but they would be unable to tell you how you are perceived without bias. So what do you have going for you and against you? See if you can figure it out. It is important for a job interview and for life going forward.

SOME INTERVIEW DOs AND DON'Ts FROM THE OTHER SIDE

The following information is from an e-mail I received from a HR executive. She sent this to every recruiter she worked with because she was fed up with people and resumes that wasted her time. Here is what she had to say:

- *Know the name of the person you are interviewing with. Call ahead to get the proper pronunciation, if you need to.*
- *Do a bit of research on the company. For example: If you are interviewing at a Hedge Fund and you don't know what Private Equity means, you are probably ill-prepared.*
- *Do not arrive late. Do not arrive late. Do not arrive late. If you suspect that you will be late, reschedule your interview. If you do find yourself late, do not blame your lateness on traffic. Accept responsibility for the error, and explain that perhaps you did not realize the amount of time it would take given the time of day. Passing the buck NEVER works for an administrator. Lateness NEVER works, not for interview candidates, or for employees.*

During the Interview:

- *Arrive for your interview in corporate attire. So many applicants have arrived out of corporate attire that my policy going forward will be to turn away those applicants not attired or groomed appropriately. Everyone has a personal style. An interview is not the time to flaunt it. Understated works best. Let me concentrate on what you are saying, and not be distracted by the day glow nail polish, glittery top, or hot pink glossy lips.*
- *Do not chew gum, do not bring your own Starbucks, or expect to extensively spruce yourself up in our restroom upon your arrival. Walk in ready for your interview.*
- *We are actually noticing you when you are waiting in reception. Be professional at all times. Loud or extensive cell phone calls, gum chewing, excessive chattiness with our receptionist or sloppy posture could be counted against you. Same goes for the restroom cell phone calls; you never know who may be in there with you!*
- *Turn your cell phone off during an interview. Show us that the interview is your priority at the moment. If you need to check your blackberry, wait. Keeping it on the table and picking it up every time you see the light blink does not prove you important, just rude.*
- *If you are given an application to fill out do not leave anything blank. Use your best handwriting and take your time to make certain everything is correct, neat, and coherent. If you rush and your application is a mess with blanks and not done to the best of your ability, it will count it against you. Use your resume to make sure everything corresponds.*
- *DO NOT make your first question about the opportunity for advancement.*

- *DO NOT talk about salary, benefits, or vacation time on your first interview.*
- *DO NOT tell me that you are "not in the market, but I received a cold call, and figured, why not?" (You would not believe how MANY candidates say just that!)*

After the Interview:

- *If you send a follow-up email, check the spelling, grammar, and the names of the individuals you refer to before you hit SEND. (I recently was working up a potential offer letter for a lady who lost the job due to her follow-up email.)*
- *Be prepared to provide references; if we ask for your references and it takes you a day to put them together, we may consider that you were not truly serious about your job search and that you began the process without adequate preparation or consideration.*

"Finally, I have a good relationship with your recruiting agent. If they make a suggestion, listen."
-Anonymous (HR Manager of a NYC Hedge Fund)

Answers to tough questions: Who can say for sure?
I recently went to Barnes and Noble and saw a book that was titled *202 Interview Questions*. It had questions *and* answers. It actually got me angry. NO ONE should be put under pressure and be told how to answer a question. Someone is asking YOU a question. You should answer it with your own mind and in your own words. Anyway, no one is so good at answering questions that their answers should be written down in a book and be repeated on an interview. Recruiters interview...yes...but we are **not** the ones *being* interviewed. I have been on just three interviews in my life. I was hired all three times and most of the reasons why can be found in the ABC chapter.

I would rather have you read what recent interviewees (both who got the job and lost the job) have to say. It is a better way to learn. Hear what they feel worked and what did not.

"First thing, SMILE on your way in! If you are sitting down, stand and shake hands with a sincere smile when the person walks in! Be 'dressed for success.' First impressions stick."
-Renee D.

"Being better prepared made me more comfortable and relaxed in my interviews because I was more confident. I did well in the interview, because I took the time to dig up a little information on the firm (through their website) and on the woman I was interviewing with. Within two days I had a job offer."
-Bill H.

"I recently lost a good job opportunity. The job was a receptionist at a small company. I asked if there was room for advancement. I wanted to show them I was interested in not just being a receptionist all my life and I was ambitious. That was not what they wanted to hear and I knew it because the interview changed after I asked that question, I could feel it. I did not know why."
-Kendra P.

Well Kendra, I know why...the company needed a receptionist, not a receptionist that was going to ask about a raise or a better position soon after starting. First get your foot in the door, work your butt off, make the company function better with you there and *then* ask for a raise or a more involved position. Many people ask that question in an interview thinking it is a smart move that proves ambition.

All it proves is you want instant gratification. It is not what the interviewer wants to hear. Don't make this mistake. (More on this in the next chapter.) Instead *show* what you can do first and work your tail off at the job. Be offered this job and *own* that job for a while, then you have a right to ask that question. On an interview, you only have a right to ask questions that pertain to the job they are interviewing you for. That is ultimately what you are there for.

"Arrive on time, dressed in corporate attire. This is very important. I feel that many employers will judge a candidate just on their arrival time and their appearance. I would add that men should wear a tie to an interview.

"Be professional at all times. This is also extremely important. Personally, I turn my cell-phone, iPod, etc. off as soon as I arrive to an interview and put it away in my bag. There's no reason to be on the phone or to be using any other gadget when you are waiting to be interviewed.

"Also, your body language and whether or not you are attentive to the interviewer's questions are all very important, too. It has helped me in the past to be aware of sitting with good posture, not to fidget in my seat or slouch, not to begin my sentences with "umm..." or "like..." or "you know." Employers want to see a candidate who has self-confidence and is able to speak clearly and without nervousness.

"This is one last thing I wanted to add on my own. I read an article on CareerJournal.com recently stating that since social networking sites (e.g. www.Facebook.com) have become popular, candidates are sending follow-up emails via the social networking sites. This is a huge No-No. *Do Not look up your interviewer and add them as your Facebook.com friend or send a thank you note to them through these websites. It crosses the boundaries of personal/professional conduct."*

-Gregory S.

"Know what the company does, how your role will fit into the grand scheme, etc. If you can't find this information out by researching, then you already have topics of discussion for your interview. Also, it is very important that you emphasize that you are interviewing for a position that interests you, it is important for the hiring personnel to know that this is the job you really want. Be sure to interview with confidence and knowing that you belong with the company and that you are the best candidate, and you should be well on your way to success."

-Robert M.

"The interviewing process is tedious and exhausting. Repeating everything over and over is hard work but you have to remember the person in front of you DOES NOT know you and has never heard what YOU have to say. Even if you are tired or simply tired of the process you cannot show that to your interviewer. You have to act fresh as if this is your very first interview There are many things you can do to get yourself ready for an interview but I think all will fall into place if you walk into the interview refreshed and feeling like a million dollars. You should not book your interviews back-to-back. Give yourself at least 3 hours. (You never know.) And as Jill said to me many many times, walk in there 'interview ready': phone turned off (very important), groomed, confident, and prepared. You don't want to be completely ignorant as to what kind of company you are meeting with. Many times I bumped into the 'website is under construction' situation and I found www.hoovers.com is very helpful. If all fails, ask the agency. They have some information on the company."

-Caroline M.

"As a general guideline, please...use your common sense. Be polite. Be professional. And above all, be yourself. You've come a long way in the course of the past four years. After all those sleepless nights devoted to writing response papers about Post-Structuralist France and the hours you've agonized over those Statistics problem sets, you owe it to yourself to put

your best foot forward. So believe in that, believe in yourselves. If you don't, you cannot hold that accountability to anyone else. Have confidence in who you are and what you have to offer. I guarantee you, it's significant."
-Laurel H.

"Arrive 10 minutes early and always speak articulately (which means, remove the word "like" from your vocabulary! You'll sound like a college student hanging out in the cafeteria. Think before you speak and speak slowly if that helps. Prep with your recruiters as much as you can because they have information that is crucial for your interview. They will also give you advice as to how to answer tricky questions. (Example: "What is your biggest weakness?") Always follow-up with your recruiter after the interview is over. Call him/her to let them know how it went; they will be waiting. It is also good to ask questions as well during an interview, because the interviewer will ask you if you have any. Your recruiter could give you some good suggestions, but one that has worked well for me are "What does it take to be successful in your company?" Be polite with everyone you meet. Stand up to shake someone's hand if a new person enters the room. Greet and thank the receptionist. Say thank you to the person who brings you water. NO CELL PHONE ANYWHERE. Save that for when you are out of the building! No texting in the reception area either. Turn it off completely. It's better to be safe than sorry."
-Ilka H.

Pet peeves
So there it is from recent interviewees. Heed their advice. But I told you that as a recruiter, I hear both sides. So, I informally polled Partners, HR Managers, and Administrators in New York City and compiled a top ten list of their pet peeves regarding the people they interview.

Here is what they said were the 10 most frustrating things about interviewing job seekers:

10. Being rude to the receptionist, door man, or test administrator.
9. Not filling out the application correctly or completely.
8. Saying negative things about prior places of employment, management, or co-workers.
7. Not asking questions during the interview about the job itself.
6. Being dressed inappropriately
5. Improper use of the English language.
4. Asking about other openings in the company, not the one they are interviewing for.
3. Interrupting the interviewer by cutting in while they are speaking.
2. Not answering their questions in a direct manner and/or changing the subject. (NOT LISTENING.)
1. Not researching the company beforehand and knowing about the company itself.

Two other things that came up again and again, but didn't make the list were no eye contact and heavy cologne or perfume. So look 'em in the eye and knock it off with the perfume and cologne (you know who you are).

A few other areas that need to be addressed:

The Handshake
If you have a good solid handshake then you know all about the "wet noodle" or "dead fish." Most people wince inside when we get those handshakes. Be aware of the way you are shaking someone's hand. I have never shaken a hand that was limp and thought the person it belonged to was a viable candidate. To me, their mind was exactly like their handshake: WEAK.

When you hold your hand out to someone, be strong and confident about touching the other person's hand. When I get a solid and firm *(but not too strong)* handshake, I feel confidence from the person I am shaking hands with.

If you squeeze too hard with numerous up and down shakes, you are going to come off as too strong and annoying. Also, don't go in too fast and grab someone's fingers for the shake. That is annoying. Pay attention, lock hands comfortably but firmly; give two easy pumps with eye-to-eye contact the entire time and boom: you're done. A genuine smile won't hurt along with it, either. This needs to be natural. Practice it a few times with a few different people and it will become like second nature.

"Many years ago, as part of my first position as a secretary in a regional state office of the New York State Office of Economic Opportunity, I was asked to attend a statewide conference at Oneonta College. The Director of one of the regional offices was to speak at the conference. During the welcome cocktail hour, I was introduced to this woman and of course, I extended my hand. As she held my hand, she looked at me point blank and said 'Young lady, don't ever offer such a limp handshake. When you shake someone's hand, you must be firm and direct and sure of yourself. I have never and will never forget that. *My handshake was what I thought it should be, respectful of her and meek. But it showed me to be weak and I should not be perceived that way. I never did that again. It was good advice."*
-Sandy S. (Administrative Assistant at a highly competitive liberal arts college)

Oh and if you have sweaty palms, keep some disposable alcohol wipes in your pocket. If you rub your hands with the alcohol before an interview, it will keep them dry and you will feel more confident.

The Thank You Note
This may sound crazy, but I know applicants who have been offered a job over another similarly qualified candidate simply because they sent a beautifully hand written note after the interview and other applicant did not. They sent a Thank You note or e-mail to every person that they met with when they interviewed. I also know others who lose offers because they misspelled the person's name they met with in the note or because they used poor grammar in their note.

"When sending a follow up email or a thank you email be careful. This was actually an issue I had personally that almost cost me my current position. I did not do a grammar check before sending out my email. I also had a philosophical quote that appeared at the end of my email right under my signature. Apparently, this was a big no-no as well. After some carefully crafted damage control by Jill, this issue was rectified, however, I absolutely lucked out. Most people-hiring, especially at such prestigious companies, would never be that understanding. It is important to be very meticulous with these follow-up emails. Sometimes people looking for a job might put a huge emphasis on the interview and completely disregard how much emphasis is to be placed on the "Thank you" email. You must pay attention to every last detail."
-Sonya K.

Here's a good tip: Whomever you interview with, ask them for a business card. Now you have their name spelled correctly, their e-mail address, and mailing address. You are now completely covered for the Thank You note or e-mail.

Beware of the "Nice" Interviewer
If I had a dollar for every time this next example happened to me I'd be rich. A job candidate for a job opening goes in for an interview and meets with an HR

executive that is super sweet, very easy to talk, down to earth, kind, and accommodating. Then, the applicant (who is feeling very comfortable) lets their guard down and ends up talking about their cat or their family or whatever. Or worse, they get into a heart-to-heart about something devastating that happened to them or their friend such as an illness or something tragic. After the interview the job seeker calls me and says: "That went great. We talked about so much personal stuff, we didn't even get to discuss work. She loved me. I told her all about my trip to England and how I met my husband and her husband is from England, could you believe it? Anyway, we *really hit it off*, so much to talk about I didn't want to leave. I think I aced it!"

Then the client calls. "Jill, she was very nice but not really the right fit. I really need someone who is a little more focused and goal-oriented. Do you have any other candidates?" Ok, now let me point out here, the women she felt was *not the right fit* had every last qualification and requirement for the job opening. EVERY LAST ONE! Ah! I could scream.

"I was interviewing a candidate for a teaching a position. She was terrific--both qualified and poised. We were having a great conversation. Somehow we ventured onto the topic of gambling. All of the sudden, she blurted out with laughter that she once lost ALL her money on one bet in Vegas. Her parents had to wire her money just so she could get back home! She was irresponsible to do something so off-the-cuff. Who would do that? I didn't hire her."

-John F. (Principal)

Point is: Do not forget you are on an interview, not even for one second. Be kind and make small talk but keep it *small*. Don't tell them EVERYTHING. Tell them some things. And pick and choose wisely. This is not a bonding session. This is an interview. Be very careful what you let the interviewer know about you and your experiences. Those things *prove* something about you.

Remember, if you are doing most of the talking and the interviewer is just smiling and nodding and looking at you, it is probably not the ideal situation.

- You need to be aware of what you are saying and how they are reacting.
- Be concise and do not ramble.
- Keep your responses short (three or four sentences).
- Do not monopolize the conversation.
- And do not think for one minute they have decided to offer you a job because you two are laughing together. They haven't, but laughing together is a good start. But it's just a start!

Chapter Seven

Q&A

No one interviews for a living, including those "experts" who have written books about interviewing. Yes, I interview people for a living, but I do not GET interviewed for a living. I do not know what the correct response is for every question asked. No one should claim to know what an interviewer wants to hear. Telling someone exactly how to respond to a question is a bunch of bull.

I may give advice on responding to questions, such as "Always include something about the company in your response," but I will never sit down and tell an applicant about what questions to expect and to prepare for in an interview. The reason is that any practiced answer is going to sound rehearsed and fake. It will be immediately apparent to the interviewer and turn them off. Focus on your ABCs and give thoughtful honest answers.

Please do not buy books or look on-line and find questions that employers may ask as part of an interview and memorize the answers. The interviewer KNOWS you memorized the answers to those questions. We know when answers are rehearsed and when they are genuine. How do we know? Again, it is our job to know. Plus someone just came in before you with the same answer that you said. It's not hard.

"Many people ask the same thing. I don't know where they are getting these questions. It is annoying because it sounds so rehearsed. When I hear a sharp, genuine question about the company, it starts a dialogue between us. I am totally engaged in the interview. They just hooked me on their line. Now, can they reel me in? But honestly, if they just researched how to interview and what to ask and did not look into our company, they lose me. I know they are not really interested in us; they want a paycheck and a job for now."
-Maria D.

However, I am more than happy to provide input on the questions that YOU should ask your prospective employer during an interview. Even better is what you SHOULD NOT EVER ask during an interview.

Below are ***Twelve Of The Worst Questions*** to ask an employer on a job interview. In case you might disagree, I have included what the interviewer is probably thinking after you ask them.

#12
Question: When are paychecks given...weekly or bi-weekly?
They're Thinking: Um...how about never?

#11
Question: Is there a lot of downtime? Because I like to stay busy.
They're Thinking: Great! As soon as you get disinterested, you'll quit or get a better job and then I will have to re-fill this job again! NEXT!

#10
Question: What is the company policy on lateness or absence?
They're Thinking: Why? Do you plan on being late and absent often?

#9
Question: What is the pay?
They're Thinking: That's funny! I don't remember mentioning that I wanted to hire you.

#8
Question: How much vacation time is allowed for this position?
They're Thinking: Two weeks. Let me guess: you don't think that's enough, right?

#7
Question: How long are lunch breaks?
They're Thinking: Lunch breaks? Well let's see...most days we all scarf down lunch at our desks and then by 3 pm, when we can't stand being cooped up any longer and our brain is fried, we go out for five minutes to get coffee.

#6
Question: When will I know if I got the job or not?
They're Thinking: I have no idea...but how about never.

#5
Question: What do you offer in terms of benefits?
They're Thinking: I'm sorry. I don't recall making you an offer.

#4
Question: Are other people interviewing for this position?
They're Thinking: No. We programmed everything we needed for a new employee into our special computer system and it spit out your name and telephone number. You are it.

#3
Question: How long was the last person in this job before it became open?
They're Thinking: Are you fishing to see how crappy the job is or are you just stupid?

#2
Question: Is there opportunity for advancement and if so, after how long?
They're Thinking: You haven't even showed up for a day of work at THIS position and you are asking about moving up? Are you kidding me? I myself am still waiting for a promotion!

#1
Question: How long before a raise is given or more vacation time is permitted?
They're Thinking: *How long?* How long must I keep pretending you have a chance at getting this job without being rude and ending the interview?

All these questions have one thing in common. They are all about the job seeker and what the company is going to do for them. When the job is **offered** then all these questions can be asked. With an offer, the job seeker has earned the right to ask whatever questions he or she wishes. The answers will help them make the decision whether or not to accept the position.

Here are the ***Top Ten Best Questions*** to ask an employer on an interview. Included, as before, are what they are probably thinking.

#10
Question: In your opinion what are the common qualities of the best employees?
They're Thinking: This person wants to be a good employee and is asking for a few pointers.

#9
Question: What is the organizational structure of this company?
They're Thinking: This person is interested in knowing who's who in the company and how we work together.

#8
Question: If I have questions about a job task or need advice, who is the best person to ask for help?
They're Thinking: They want to know who the correct person is to ask for advice. They know not to ask just anyone. They want the correct information and they are willing to ask for help, but don't want to annoy the wrong person. Nice.

#7
Question: Are new hires given any training when they begin working here?
They're Thinking: Training is important to them. They know they will need it to do a good job here.

#6
Question: What can a new employee do in order to adapt quickly to your company?
They're Thinking: This person wants to fit in here.

#5
Question: How early do employees arrive in the office and how late do they leave?
They're Thinking: This person isn't thinking "9 to 5" and will probably be the first one in and the last one out.

#4
Question: How do employees make management's job easier and what makes a supervisor's job more difficult?
They're Thinking: A brown-nose question but still...how to be a low maintenance employee makes my job easier. Points!

#3
Question: Do the employees ever get together outside of the office?
They're Thinking: This person wants a home. They want to get together with their co-workers outside work and get to know them.

#2

Question: What do you feel are the most important things to do in the first few months of being hired for this position?

They're Thinking: This person wants to hit the ground running.

AND THE NUMBER ONE MOST IMPORTANT QUESTION:

#1

Question: The one you make up yourself. Ask a specific question that PROVES you did research on the company. You'll need to do research in order to figure out what that question will be. It will be different for every interview and each company.

They're Thinking: This person did their homework, More points!

All of *these* questions have one thing in common. They are all about the company and what the applicant can do for the company or for other employees. They have nothing to do with the individual.

So my fellow job seekers:
ASK NOT WHAT YOUR EMPLOYER CAN DO FOR YOU, ASK WHAT *YOU* CAN DO FOR YOUR EMPLOYER.

When on the interview, you should not ask all ten questions. Asking too many questions will sound rehearsed. Perhaps choose two or three and see where the interviewer's answers takes the conversation. How the interviewer answers these questions will tell you if there is a good chance at getting an offer. When these questions produce elaborate responses, it's a good sign. If they bring one or two word answers, you probably are not going to get an offer of employment.

3 Tricky Questions from Employers

1. What is your biggest weakness?

They may as well just say this: *Tell me something about yourself that doesn't include praise.*

A tip on answering this question: do not make it in regard to you as an employee, make it in regard to you as an individual. Then just tell the truth. *Make small talk, not BIG TALK.*
Example: "I am often concerned about fitting in and what others think of me" or "I hate to work out." Keep it personal.

Note: What do you do if they ask, "What is your biggest weakness as an employee?" *I can't and won't tell you what to say, but I will give you a HINT: I am sure you try your best not to have a biggest weakness, right? Whatever mistakes you make, you correct, before they get BIG. Give an example of something that could have been BIG that you corrected and tried to fix.*

2. How did you deal with a problem in your past work environment?

I love asking this and I always do. Here is your chance to prove something about your ABCs. Remember your ABCs when answering this question and answer it truthfully. Did you ever have a circumstance at work where you needed to problem-solve fast, under pressure? Or did you ever have to grin and bear it and keep working even when you were fed up? This is the perfect time to interject the fact that you are a good worker. Take the ball and run with it here.

3. What do you feel is your goal in the next few years?
They may as well say, "How long are you going to stay with us before I have to refill this position?" They are giving you a chance here to sink or swim. I will not tell you how you should answer these questions, but I will tell you a few rules when answering anything concerning longevity and your plan for your future.

1. Remember your audience AND THEIR GOAL for the next few years (which is probably to hire a good staff that stays with the company and makes the company run better).
2. Keep your answers small. Again, make small talk, not big talk.
3. Keep the *industry* and you tied together in your answer.

Also do not be afraid to say, "I am not sure." That is a fair answer. But tie yourself to WORKING and to making a living and having a career and an apartment and a life in that area. That is what they want to hear. That is truthful and it ties to you the need for a job with them.

THEY DO NOT WANT TO HEAR THAT YOU REALLY WANT TO BE IN A DIFFERENT LINE OF WORK BUT THIS IS WHERE YOU HAVE TO START. (Ahh! You better not say that.)

In the end, remember to listen and be in the moment. It is the one thing that is guaranteed to make the interview go smoother, because it ensures that the conversation will be better from the interviewer's point of view. It can make the Ivy League summa cum laude graduate lose the job to the Community College graduate. It is the single most important way to show you have *IT*.

Chapter Eight

THE TESTS

"When I first met with Jill she gave me typing, Word, and Excel tests. Based on my test scores, Jill was able to pinpoint which jobs I'd be well suited for, and which not. We focused on a few employers that were looking for someone with my skills and experiences, rather than a bunch of employers for whom I would be under- or over-qualified. This saved me time and allowed me to better prepare for the jobs I was a good match for.

"Within a couple days, Jill got me an interview. The employer gave me a typing and Word test. I did very well on them because I was confident and prepared from the tests I had taken with Jill."

-Bill H.

MS Word, Excel, PowerPoint

This is where you should shine like the sun. You have never known the world without a computer and you should get 100% on these tests. People who are only 10 years older than you do not have the experience and advantages that you've had with Microsoft Office products. Your generation usually does better cold on these tests than your average 30- or 40-year-old. If you ace them, that is a huge advantage.

However some people think they are experts, but do not score well on the test. Many people do not do tasks the correct way, the way the engineers of MS Word intended, so that all workers are on the same page and have a universal code or style of working with a document. A company is giving you a test to see if you do your own thing (like *tab* through everything) or if you can truly format a document the correct way. It is important to be aware of these questions and make sure you know how to do these functions in *MS Word, PowerPoint* and *Excel* correctly.

Also: find out how to link the programs. If you are working on Word do you know how to insert an Excel spreadsheet into your Word document? If you don't know...learn. If you don't have related work experience, you can often make up for that with a proficiency in these software programs.

You know it? ... Prove it!

The web site www.ProveIt.com is devoted to test questions on varies software applications for Microsoft Word Office Suite. They also include tests for typing, spelling and grammar and so many other options for possible tests given on computers at a job site.

Below are a list of common tasks and functions found in MS Word, Excel, and PowerPoint. Use this list of functions from.*PROVE IT.com* to freshen up your skills.

If you do not know how to accomplish any of these functions go to HELP on the corresponding program and type in the topic. It will explain how to do it correctly.

On the next page we will outline the main functions in three major softeware programs: MS Word, Excel, and PowerPoint. You may see how many of these you are already familiar with or have expertise in.

MS Word Functions

1. Opening a Document
2. Save As
3. Typing in a Document
4. Select Text
5. Font Face
6. Font Size
7. Italics
8. Underlining
9. Centering
10. Tracking Changes
11. Cutting Text
12. Pasting
13. Insert a Picture
14. Numbering Pages
15. Inserting the Date
16. Replace Productivity Tools
17. Spell Check
18. Columns
19. Margins
20. Print Preview
21. Printing
22. Switch Between Documents
23. Macros
24. Insert a Table
25. Copying
26. Sorting
27. View as a Web page
28. Open a blank Document
29. Create Merge Mailing Labels
30. Closing Word

Excel Functions

1. Opening Workbook
2. Insert Rows
3. Cutting and Pasting Text
4. Center Across Columns
5. Editing Cells
6. Text Wrap
7. Text Alignment
8. Font/Font Size
9. Font Style
10. Format Number
11. Save
12. Selecting Cells
13. Borders
14. Print Scaling
15. Navigating in a Worksheet
16. Use SUM Function
17. Paste a Function
18. Column Width
19. Insert Column
20. Use AVERAGE Function
21. Insert Worksheet
22. Renaming a Worksheet
23. Insert Chart
24. Page Orientation
25. Margins
26. Header/Footer
27. Print Center on Page
28. Spell Check
29. Save As
30. Print Worksheet

PowerPoint Functions

1. New Presentation
2. Add Text to a Slide
3. Inserting Slides
4. Demoting Points
5. Applying a New Presentation Design
6. Inserting Pictures
7. Editing text
8. Slide Navigation
9. Bold
10. Slide Master
11. Changing Views
12. Rearranging Slides
13. Adding Transitions
14. Adding Animations
15. Set Automatic Slide Timings
16. Moving Objects
17. Group objects
18. Inserting Organizational Chart
19. Adding a Subordinate
20. Insert Note
21. Hide Slide
22. Insert Chart
23. Animate Chart
24. Deleting Slides
25. Drawing Object
26. Changing Border Color
27. Inserting Page Numbers
28. Save As
29. Run Slide Show
30. Print Outline View
31. Setting Properties
32. Change Slide Color Schemes

33. Change Background
34. Change Slide Layout
35. Style Checker
36. Inserting WordArt
37. Modifying WordArt
38. Create AutoShape
39. Modify AutoShape
40. Change Chart Type
41. Chart Options
42. Insert Movie Clip
43. Apply Animation Scheme
44. Apply Custom Animation
45. Continuous Play
46. Slides from Presentations
47. Insert Excel Worksheet
48. Edit Worksheet
49. Save as Web Page
50. Save as PowerPoint Show
51. Print Handout

Typing
People between the age of 20 and 30 have been typing ever since grade school. They should be able to type 50+ words per minute.

Without practice most people over 35 years of age cannot type nearly as fast as those between 20 and 30. I can not count how many times a twenty-something job seeker came into my office and responded "I don't know" when I asked their typing speed. Then they type 80 words per minute CLEAN... not one error. That is amazing!

Then I test an experienced secretary of 20 years. They might type 50 words per minute with five errors and say, " I am rusty." It happens to me every day. Some experienced secretaries do type well, but almost all younger grads type fast.

If your resume states: *Excellent MS Word, PowerPoint, and Excel skills*, you'd better ace the tests. If you wrote 60 words per minute typing, you'd better be able to type 60 words per minute with no errors or better. If you do well in every other area during an interview, but your claims on your resume do not match your test scores, you're toast. You will not get the job.

Ladies: cut your fingernails if typing is part of your job. Your long fingernails will slow you down on tests so get rid of them before you interview. I have seen people chewing them off their hands while sitting in the testing room in my office because they can't get a decent score on the typing test.

To practice and to get your score, go to www.***typingtudor.com*** or www.***typingtests.com***

The Test Giver
The person giving you these tests at the company or the agency should be treated with the utmost respect and kindness. If you gain points with them right off the bat and get them in your corner, you are much better off.

- Do not complain to these people; do not be rude or ask for a quieter space to test.
- Everyone tests in the same place and you must go with the flow.
- Do not under any circumstance get up and leave. Finish and do the best you can. If you have to leave, change your other plans. Figure out a way to stay and finish the test. If you walk away, the entire interview is over. You will not get the job.

"Your candidate came in here and aced the tests, but the entire time she was testing she complained about the testing area, the test itself, and the noise in the hallway. We will pass on her, thank you."
-HR Coordinator NYC Law firm

Even during the tests, you are being interviewed for the job. The interview process stops when you get the job. Not a moment before. Oh! And then on your first day at work, you start interviewing again, now with co-workers and management and clients. So it never really stops. Interviews are given so a company can see how you handle yourself. Essentially, you will use your interview skills (your ABCs) every day of your working career.

Chapter Nine

THE CALL-BACK AND THE OFFER

Preparing For The Second Interview
When you get a call to return for another interview, you have to gather information for this interview once again.

The "Call-Back" Interviewers
Find out all the people with whom you will be meeting with. Yes—all of them. And what are their titles at the office. Then do your homework again. You can look them up online: either Google them or go to the company's web site to try and find some information on them. If you cannot find anything specific about them, then simply research the department they work in and find out all you can. Also find out about both the company and the *industry*. Ask questions that prove you did your research. The people you meet on a call-back interview are the ones to impress with your knowledge about the industry, not just their company. Prove you did your homework and be able to discuss the industry intelligently. And remember if you do research on *them*, do not let them know point blank that you checked them out. Doing research on them allows you to be privy to what makes them tick a little bit. The more you know about them, the more you can connect with them, but be sure to do it subtly. Don't say: "I found out this or that about you." That is borderline rude.

I can tell you for sure that you are now a viable candidate for this job. The first person that interviewed you has now referred you on. They thought you were polished and professional. You *proved* yourself and they also liked you. They are now putting their credibility on the line just by asking you to come back and meet with someone else in their company. Now you have someone on your side and for their own sake, they want you to look good when you return to their company. So, ask away. Ask them questions and tell them you'd like to be prepared. If you have a recruiter, ask the recruiter to help research this information. Ask questions about what is expected of the person for this position. Ask anything you'd like about the future of business for the company and how your position, no matter how small, can make a difference. Ask away...BUT...still...

- Do not ask about salary.
- Do not ask about vacation time.
- Do not ask about where you will sit or anything that will make you seem as though you assume you have the job. Remember: you do not have an offer yet.

References
Same as your appearance: you can't pick and choose if you will do this or not. Do it. It will prove that you think ahead and are efficient.

Create and have on hand a list of references. Have at least 3 references printed (beginning with the most recent) on the same grade paper as your resume. Use the same paper, the same format, and the same font as you used in your resume. Include the following information for each reference:

- Name of person you *worked under* (Do not write down names of co-workers; you need a manager or someone in charge of you.)
- Their phone number *during business hours*

- Their current title and current place of employment
- Their title and place of employment at the time you worked together (if it is different from their current job)

I get this question all the time. Can I list a Professor? Yes, Yes and Yes! Professors are great references, absolutely! But try to put just one. Make sure this professor is someone who is enthusiastic and will gladly speak on your behalf. I like speaking to a professor for a reference on one of their former students. It makes me want to help the applicant even more by the time I hang up the phone. Speaking to a professor who truly cares about a particular student is heartwarming. This student stood out to them somehow and it says something about their ABCs.

When you interview, take three to four copies of your resume and three or four copies of your references. Do not hand over your references unless someone asks you for them. This shows you are prepared and confident. Handing off a list of references when no one asked you for them shows you are falling back on them because you feel you have nothing else. It also shows you are not following the interviewers lead. Believe me: let them ask *you* for references and then come out winning and impressive by having a typed list on good paper for their file.

But before you hand over that list you **better have called everyone on it** and told him or her you were putting them down as a reference. You better have made sure all the information is absolutely correct: phone number, title, and current place of employment. And most importantly you should make certain they will give you a good reference. Too many times in my career, I have lost a deal because of a bad reference. Funny thing is the applicant provided the reference himself or herself. Ahh! That drives me nuts.

One bad reference and you lost all your chips at the casino; you're done. Your job interview and offer is now gone and your recruiter probably won't work with you again. If you are not sure if someone will give you a solid reference get hold of them on the phone and ask point blank. "*I am trying for a job at a great company. If I list your name as a reference will you give me a positive recommendation?*" If they are on the fence about it, do not list them. If they sound excited and happy to do it, you will hear it in their voice. You should know who would give you a solid reference. You *know* because you worked with them and have *experience* with that person. That's right; you *know*.

Call-back Questions

The people you meet on the second (or call back) interview are the stars of this interview not you. Let them lead the conversation. Let them tell you what they need, what they want and how they want it done. Again: jot down information on a note pad of the important things they say (pick and choose what is important to write down—not everything will be).

If they ask you anything about you, keep it as professional as possible and remember make *small* talk not big talk. Also, go back to the Top 10 List and try to create a few of the number-one questions: the ones you make up yourself. Have three of those up your sleeve and you will be golden. In the call-back interview all questions asked should be ones you make up yourself from the research you did on the company or the person you are meeting with.

Appearance—Again!
You thought you looked great last time you went in to interview? I challenge you to look even better for the call back. Work out for a week, eat right, drink lots of water, and get lots of rest. Diet. Get a facial. Get your hair cut or done. Spend time and money to look amazing, even better than before. Step it up a notch and believe me, it will help you inside and out.

The Offer
They offered you a job. Ask away. Ask everything you wanted to before but did not. Ask about the vacation time given. The medical, dental, 401k, and when would those benefits start: after 90 days or as soon as you start the job? Ask about salary and the opportunity for overtime (and what overtime pay would be). Ask about a lunch hour and ask about a bonus at the end of the year. Also tell them about any vacation plans that are coming up and or days you need to take off.

Salary
When applying for a job, it is likely that you will know the salary range being offered for the position from the job description. Hopefully it included salary. Always expect to be offered the minimum within that range.

Never, ever be the first to give a specific salary amount. Always say and write (on the application) one word: Negotiable. Let them say a dollar amount when the time comes. They are offering you a job, after all. They decided they want you to work there. If you are pushed for a dollar amount, ask what they usually offer people in your category. Again: press them back for a dollar amount and go from there.

Larger companies usually do an analysis about what salary to offer incoming staff members. So you will be offered pretty much what everyone else was offered. If the company is smaller you had *better follow every rule in this book* to make sure you came off polished and professional. With small and mid-size companies, those things will help with salary negotiation. The better you looked, spoke, and presented yourself, the higher your offer will be.

Accept the job if you can swing it financially as long as the salary is at least 5K over minimum wage, if you have a college degree. If you live in a large city make that 10k over minimum wage. If you don't have a college degree and this company provides 401k and all types of benefits **take the job** even if the salary is minimum wage. Why? Because of the opportunity and the chance to get started in the industry. After a year or two you can move to a new company if you feel like you can not live on that income. But honestly, if you cannot swing it on the money they offered, why did you interview with them in the first place?

Another important question to ask: Is the salary exempt or would you have the opportunity to earn overtime pay? (If a salary is *exempt* it means you do not have the opportunity to earn overtime. The company feels the overtime pay is included in the base salary.) If the salary is NOT exempt and you are able to make overtime pay after 35 or 40 hours, that makes a big difference. According to most state laws, an employer must pay an overtime rate of *time and a half* per hour for any hours worked over 40 in a week. Some companies offer overtime pay after only 35 hours a week. Example: If you earn equivalent to $10 an hour and work 45 hours that week then you should be paid 40 hours at $10 and 5 hours at $15 per hour.

So remember if a large company offers you what you feel is too low a salary and you cannot live on that kind of money, then ask about the possibility of working overtime. This can be a huge factor when trying to determine how much money you can earn with this employer. But if you want the job and you do take it at a low salary you will be working your way up to more money and better perks in the long run. So if you have a chance to get into a large corporation grab it.

Remember this is a STARTING salary and position....
Read this message from someone who was a college graduate placed as a secretary whose intelligence and work history surpassed the qualifications for this entry-level position.

"They know you are smarter than that. The company who hired you knows that you are smarter than just someone who is there to answer phones and type or do Internet research. But they still want you to doing these tasks. But don't fall into that and pigeon-hole yourself. Get out there and work hard and stay late with the higher-ups in your company. Soon you'll be going to lunch with those people. If you are a dedicated hard worker and you prove it, in the long run you will be accepted no matter what your title."
-David G.

Jill DeSena-Shook

Chapter Ten

STAYING POWER

Once you accept the job and the salary is agreed upon - you will get a start date. When you arrive at the company for your first day of work, you are beginning 90 days of more interviews. The only way to *prove* anything about yourself is through your ABC's. Keep in mind that your attitude, behavior and character matter as much as job performance. Every company that has ever achieved anything has standards. You have to *prove* that your attitude behavior and character matches those of your co-workers and the ideals of the company. This will allow you to focus on a common goal and trust one another while working.

Probation

Whether formally or informally, you will be on probation. It doesn't matter if it is verbally expressed or written in the employee handbook or not, every new employee is on probation for at least the first 90 days. Yes, that is correct: even you with the 4.0 GPA and Ivy League degree, you are on probation, too.

You accepted a job and the company accepted you, but that doesn't mean every employee at the company accepts you. For the first few months you will be informally "re-interviewed" by each and every individual that you meet. No one is going to tell you this when you start a job. In fact, if you ask anyone they will probably tell you just the opposite and say, "Oh this is such a wonderful place to work, with wonderful people; we all get along great!" I can tell you from experience that this is hardly ever the truth. There is at least one in every crowd who will be a jerk if given the chance, so be on your best behavior.

Get up early and get to work early and keep yourself healthy at all costs. Don't party too much and get a good night's sleep each night. If your initial work performance is not up to par, but your attendance and punctuality are perfect, they will not let you go during the probationary period. Why? They know you are trying. The company (if it is worth staying with) will work with you and help you do well. But, if you are out of the office and late all the time in the first few months they will actually *look* for reasons to let you go.

Ninety days' probation includes more than just no absence and no lateness. It also includes:

- No gossiping
- No long lunches
- No dating co-workers. I repeat: *No dating co-workers.*
- No bad language
- No discussing salaries
- No crude jokes
- No heavy drinking at holiday parties (two is enough!)
- No Internet on the job (Unless it is FOR the job)
- No ethnic, sexist, or religious comments
- No brown nosing the boss
- No doctor/dentist/OB-GYN appointments on work days

Being Late or Out Sick
Lateness and absence is something that for the most part is within your control. Not being there on time *proves* you don't want to be there. Period. You must be at work, on time, every single day. In the morning, leave extra early to ensure that you'll be on time. Do a dry run beforehand so you know for sure where the company is located. Traffic, train problems, and "I lost my wallet" will not work. It will seem like these excuses work, but I promise you that it is tucked away in the mind of your boss and co-workers. If it happens more than three times - you are on thin ice. Remember that *entitled* stereotype? It doesn't go away once you get hired.

To summarize: Do not be out sick or late for *at least* three months after you start the job. Let me repeat that for those of you who read it, but did not really want to believe it: DO NOT BE OUT SICK OR LATE FOR *AT LEAST* THREE MONTHS AFTER YOU START THE JOB!

Vacations
If you have vacation plans or need a day off within the first few months of your start date, tell your new employer WHEN YOU AGREE TO THE SALARY, *BEFORE* YOU START. DO NOT TELL THEM ON YOUR FIRST DAY OF WORK OR THE WEEK BEFORE YOU NEED THE TIME OFF. THAT IS UNPROFESSIONAL AND WILL BE FROWNED UPON.

Doctor's Appointments
That's right: tell the doc you just started a new job and get a Saturday appointment. If they don't have Saturday appointments or any after work hours, then you must go to another doctor. Your job is too important to risk taking time-off during your probation. Why? If everyone took all their doctor's appointments during business hours, no one would be at work. They'd all be at the doctor's office.

This job is not about you and your schedule. It is about the company and the hours you agreed to work for them. Your new employer will never tell you what I am telling you. They will say, "sure, no problem" or "that's fine." Guess what? It's *not* fine. You just started the job and unless you told the boss about this appointment before you accepted the job, you will look unprofessional by making a doctor's appointment during business hours. Don't do it.

Dress Appropriately and Adapt to the Corporate Culture
Your co-workers are the ones to watch in terms of what to wear. So take a look around the office on your first day and see what other people are wearing. Professional, corporate casual, and casual can mean different things for different companies, so dress to that standard OR BETTER. If you go just a tad bit worse you will be in trouble. Also ladies do not wear dresses that you would wear to an afternoon wedding or to church. That is not office attire. That is afternoon wedding sun-dress poke-a-dot- flowers and stripes attire. Please. It is not the look you want for an office.

Remember: PRESS EVERYTHING. Never show up to work in clothes that are not pressed, starched, and fit you correctly. Especially when casual or corporate casual is your office style, people tend to get lax with ironing their clothes. People will notice what you are wearing and it will affect you the same as your punctuality. If you are wearing wrinkled khakis and a polo shirt with a stain on the front, everyone with cleaned and pressed clothes will think you don't want to be there. Being sloppy doesn't say that you forgot to do laundry because you had a busy weekend. It says that you don't care enough to get it done.

Prove you have your life in order and show that in your appearance. If you are dressed impeccably, everything thing else that you do and say will be enhanced for the better.

Careful...Remember Your Audience

Remember: you really are not colleagues until you have a history together. Until you actually KNOW that person because you have EXPERIENCE with them. You don't KNOW them because you were introduced to them. KNOWING comes from EXPERIENCE. You are new to the place. You are not the person that should be cracking rude jokes or saying inappropriate things at work either about the company or the people working there. Truth is: you don't have any friends yet.

Warning

Keep this in mind if you go out with some people from the office after work. If your co-workers start talking about other people that you work with, keep your mouth shut. It is a good sign that they trust you enough to be candid in your presence, but DO NOT get involved in the gossip; it could come back to haunt you.

> I recently placed an Ivy League graduate that I will call James, at a huge well-known corporation. James said he was doing great but when it came time for the company to send me the fee for his placement at his 90 days of employment mark, they didn't. I called and asked why.
>
> The company told me that his probation was being extended. I asked why. The company couldn't say exactly but they did say they would speak to James directly.
>
> A few weeks later, James called to tell me what had happened. He was taken into human resources and told his probation was being extended for another 90 days because he passed a rude comment to a co-worker. This was not about anyone else in the office, but he said something that included a slang expression that the co-worker felt wasn't proper language for the office and the co-worker reported him to Human Resources. James told me he was shocked when the HR Manager explained why his probation was being extended. James knew who reported him and remembered this employee had said far worse things to him during the same conversation. But James remained professional and simply said, "I can not apologize enough for my poor choice of words. I can promise you that is will not happen again."
>
> He did not mention what the other employee said. That would not be professional. He realized at that very moment that he was the "new guy" and the other employee was a seasoned employee. So he apologized and promised it would not happen again. His job was saved.
>
> James stopped speaking to that co-worker because now he KNEW (that's right: he had to learn through experience) this co-worker was sneaky. Beforehand, James never imagined someone would do that to him. Now he KNOWS better.

Most people in a company would never treat a new employee that way. In my experience, that does not happen often, so please do not think that most people are sneaky. But some are and you will never be able to tell the difference until it is too late. No one is going to shake your hand and say, "Hi, watch what you say in front of me, I like to start trouble in the office, but great meeting you and have a nice first day!" You need to be AWARE that you don't KNOW people at work until you have experiences with them.

"Remember, always give your best. Never get discouraged. Never be petty. Always remember, others may hate you. But those who hate you don't win unless you hate them. And then you destroy yourself."
Richard M. Nixon (1913-1994), 37th US President (1969-74)
Resignation Address

Good Weeks & Bad Weeks
Another thing about co-workers is that you will have good weeks and bad weeks. No, I don't mean good days and bad days, I mean good weeks and bad weeks. If you have issues with someone at work it may take a while to work it out and forget it. But Friday always comes and then you have the weekend to decompress and come back fresh on Monday. As will the person who may have caused your "bad week." You will become like family with most of the people you work with. You will spend more time with your co-workers than your own family. You will come to care for them and care about them and argue with them and complain about them in ways you never would have thought possible when you started. Sometimes they will watch your back and help you, and other times they will rat you out, just like a sibling.

Everyone who has a job, a boss and co-workers has (at least once) gone into the office restroom and either cried or closed the door and wanted to scream. But instead of completely losing it, we counted to 10 and made it through. Just keep it together.

This too shall pass.

Your boss or manager—the person who hired you—may be much different toward you after you start. They may not be as nice or give you as much attention as you thought they would. Regardless of *their* ABCs, you must stay professional and not diverge from the person you were on the interview.

Is that?...WHAT ARE YOU LOOKING AT?
You BETTER NEVER EVER EVER look at porn on-line at work. The company will know. They own the computer. If you are looking, someone knows you are looking. I promise. I lost a deal not too long ago for this. The person was called into HR and had the nerve to say "I was looking up information about colon cancer." WHAT? They saw what he was looking at and there wasn't an X-Ray of an internal organ anywhere on that website. He got fired so fast it wasn't even funny. IF you think no one can see what you view at work on the Internet...you are so wrong. *Consider yourself warned.*

Also, do not give your work e-mail address to friends who will bombard you with pornographic, sexist, racist, or other extreme e-mails. You will be held accountable for any message that you open on your computer. Check emails from friends at home.

Turnaround Time
The time it takes you to finish a project, assignment or task is your turnaround time. If you made a commitment to do something at work, do not ever say to your manager the following sentence: "I didn't get to it." If you didn't get to something your boss asked for, you should say: "It will be on your desk in ____" and fill in the time-frame. *Then follow through*. Make whatever your manager askedyou're your priority. Why? Because the boss had to ask for it. One thing managers hate is when a worker agrees to a turnaround time and doesn't deliver. Or worse, not only is it not done on time; the boss had to find *you* and inquire if it was finished. *You should have come to them* to say it would be late. Maybe you thought...what?...that your manager would just forget? Did a professor ever forget a term paper was due? Right: no such luck.

If you say a project will be finished by a certain time, you'd better do it or have a good reason why it is not finished. No matter how much of a good relationship you have with your manager, you must be considerate about his or her job. Your deadlines affect management's deadlines.

Winning A Few Points
Be accommodating without being a kiss-ass. A kiss-ass is always looking for the boss. Someone accommodating and smart is always who the boss is looking for. If you want to gain a few brownie points around the office, all you have to do is get there early and leave late. Yep. That's it. Oh, and do an amazing job learning and *recalling* whatever training you were given about the company and their computer systems. People will notice that. It *proves* you WANT TO BE THERE.

A few other tips from smart people who recently got hired recently but knew their first job was not their last:

1) Have a career goal in mind (put it down on paper) and be very patient as you work incrementally towards it.
2) HOWEVER: recognize that your goals are not the same as the person who is interviewing you. Their goal is to fill a position with the best possible candidate. Listen to what they need, what their pains are, and make it your business to see that those needs are fulfilled and the pains will be healed, if they hire YOU.
3) Own every job you have. It's paying your rent, putting food on your table and clothes on your back!
4) Keep your connections, even if you think you won't need them in the future. You just never know!
5) Realize that your first job doesn't have to be your lifetime career, but it keeps your skills growing, especially if you're right out of college. Most firms are very well managed so you get fantastic knowledge of how to run an office efficiently. You also learn how to work together as a team, get great benefits (health, vision, dental, vacation, etc.), and make great friends along the way.
-David G.

"There is something that I always go back to and it's in a lot of what Jill has written. I learned it by watching a friend of mine who is an admin assistant of many years standing, but I've seen it with many other people in all lines of work and it always knocks me over when I see it because it's rarer than you might think. It's the quality of whatever is asked of me no matter how seemingly small, I will do to the best of my ability. Being on time, dressing professionally (whatever the job title might be), being forthright and pleasant is so important. I will bring my best level of professionalism to this moment and this *task. It's amazing how that attitude lifts the atmosphere, takes the task to another level. And people notice it, both coworkers and employers. It's a very powerful choice to make because it keeps*

the person doing it involved and reaching for the next level. Like a dancer who does a simple plié *and it's as graceful as a whole ballet. Well, I'm getting poetic, but you get the idea. It also has an element of humility to it, which can also be a wonderful thing. It says that even though I am qualified to do a lot more, if this is what is asked of me I can do it well. And people always always notice it."*
-Kathryn B

Going Forward...
These 5 rules from a successful client will allow you to excel in your new job and in your career going forward. No matter what your position, salary or job title, these next few tips are for your working career:

1. *Forward-think. Do your job at the level of the position you want to be in. It is not enough to just do what's asked of you. People who want to advance need to always think, "When I complete this task, what is the next thing my boss will ask me?" and have the answer ready.*

2. *Ask for projects that are a stretch for you and are at the level of the next position you want. People need to go above and beyond their job description if you want to get ahead.*

3. *Commitments and Communication! Communicate up, down, and laterally. Don't over-commit and when you do commit to something, make sure the commitments you've made are going to be met. When they are met, let people know. When you will miss,* let people know in advance. *Colleagues should not have to track you down for a status update on your project and never let someone be caught by surprise due to a lack of communication.*

4. *Be aware of "The Book" on you: no matter where you work, know that there is a book on you. It's not in writing or in your HR file, but you can be sure it's there. Think about what you want your book to say and behave to it. Remember, this is a work environment and no matter how "tight" you are with a colleague, they are still just a colleague and not your personal friend. Keep your mouth shut, keep your head down, and deliver.*

5. *Prepare and Lead. You will be invited to a number of meetings in your career. Meetings are a great place to let people you don't normally work with see your capabilities. So you need to be present and participate at every meeting. Show up prepared and be on time. Ask questions, make suggestions, but don't talk just to talk. If it's your meeting, make sure the team gets there and in the time scheduled. Tell people what you need so you walk out of the meeting having issues resolved.*

Teresa S. (Director of E-Commerce)

Are you *getting it*? Once you have completed your probation and *proven* yourself to be a competent, hard worker and a loyal employee, *only then* is your job-search complete and a good "book" is being written about you. Having a "good book" on you in the office is the way you earn respect (and a big bonus).

Jill DeSena-Shook

Afterword

10 Commandments for Success

The ideals behind the following 10 lessons are what I have learned from the time I graduated until now. They have helped me realize my own success. Had I known then what I know now (and put forth into action), I would have experienced less heartache and happier days earlier in my career and in my life.

One

From the book *You Can Heal Your Life* by Louise Hay

No one should be able to *make you feel* anything. Your feelings are completely up to you. That is power. You choose how to feel. Don't ever let anyone make that choice for you. If you have control over your moods and choose the positive your life can never be hopeless. An easy way to do this is to keep in your mind what you want, not what you don't want. Keep in your mind "I will be hired" not "No one will ever hire me."

Hay's book also taught me the way to stop getting illnesses. Mind and body are connected and one will ultimately affect the other, either toward health or disease.

Two

From *The Forum* New York City Chapter

The brain remembers events subjective to beliefs and feelings of the person it dwells in. When recalling the past there is WHAT HAPPENED and WHAT *YOU SAID* HAPPENED. Often what you *said* happened becomes your reality and it is not always the truth. Your mind has tied feelings to an event and may have altered the reality of that event.

Forgive. We as humans are not perfect. Since we may remember things incorrectly about past experiences, everyone deserves forgiveness. Start with yourself and then move on to others. Once you begin to forgive the past it gets easier to forgive yourself and others on a daily basis. If you follow this rule it will help you choose to feel good. Without even trying, you will become an example to others.

Three

From *The Four Agreements* by Miguel Ruiz

Be Impeccable with your word.
Tell the Truth.
Always.
If you mess up one day try again the next day. Keep trying every day just to consistently tell the truth. It will change your life and give you peace.

Four

A quote from *The Great Wizard of Oz*
"A heart is never judged by how much you love but by how much you are loved by others"

This means to give love away—every chance you get—to whomever you are close to and even to those you don't know yet. Whatever love you have in your heart, give it away. The way to give love away is to *show* it with your words, your actions, and your time. People will feel it and love you back simply for your effort. Showing your love genuinely will *prove* that you are worthy, having a heart. That is why it was so fitting a thing to say to the Tin Man. He asked the wizard for a heart so the wizard commented on how to use one. Using your heart to *give away* love is more important than just feeling the emotion of love towards others. This is ultimately what a "heart" is for.

Five

From the *Sermon on the Mount – Jesus of Nazareth*
"Blessed are the poor in spirit – for they shall see God."

What does it mean to be *poor in spirit*? The answer is yearning for spirit. Being "poor in" or never having enough spirit and always searching for it every minute of your life.

Whatever we truly yearn for, we will naturally seek out and claim every day. Humans are wired this way. If you yearn to have money, you will keep your money and not spend it. If you yearn for material things you will always have those things whether you have the money for them or not. If your mind truly yearns day after day for health, your body will look healthy. If your mind hungers to sit and relax and take it easy as much as you can, that is what you will do. Whatever people can never get enough of in their daily lives is what their life will become. Seek out knowledge and experiences of whatever interests you and feeds your spirit. But know that if it is wicked or selfish, it will destroy your life. If it is of goodness and decency, it will give you peace.

Six

"Are You Going to Finish Strong?"
-Nick Vujicic (Inspirational speaker)

You will fail when you try new things, but will you finish strong? You *will* go on an interview and perhaps say the wrong thing or fail the tests or simply not make a connection with the person interviewing you. If you interview one hundred times and fail, and then give up, will you EVER get a job? You must try again and again and again. You must keep your ABCs positive, especially at your worst hour. Remember, *this time in your life will pass*. Finish Strong.

(You can see Nick speak to students on line at *www.LifeWithoutLimbs.org* or on *YouTube.com.* Just type in his name.)

Seven

"I have sometimes been wildly, despairingly, acutely miserable ... but through it all I still know quite certainly that just to be alive is a grand thing."
-Agatha Christie (Best Selling Author)

You are alive. Think about it for a minute. You have hope.

Even merely taking a breath feels humbling when you appreciate just being able to so. Take a breath. That feels good, doesn't it?

Eight

From *Life's Little Instruction Book, Volume 1*
"Never Ignore Evil"

When you are good—genuinely good the way God intended you to be—be aware that not everyone else is. There is evil in the world. Don't believe that it doesn't exit. It does. Do not be afraid of it because you are always more powerful. But do not ever ignore it. Point it out and call it by name to yourself inside your head whenever you encounter it. That is the only way to keep it far away from your heart.

Nine

"Say"
-A Song by John Mayer

I am the youngest daughter of four girls. When I became an adult, I told my father that I knew he loved me, even though I was not a boy. I grew up feeling remorse that my dad never had a son. I was his last chance. He said back to me in a very matter-of-fact way, "It is irrelevant what a child 'is' when they come into the world. What sex they are or what they look like, if they are attractive or not...if they are smart or dumb, if they are fat or thin, if they are healthy or not. It is irrelevant. You came into the world as *Jill*. Jill was who I wanted. That is the way it is when you have a child. If you become a mother you will realize how foolish you were for thinking such a thing."

And to think I was caught up all my life on disappointing him. People will surprise you. Open doors of communication and "say what you need to say." Sometimes life's biggest regrets are made when you don't say what is on your mind. Time will go by and as you get older you will have more and more deep conversations with yourself and no one else.

Ten

The only thing we have to fear is fear itself.
-Franklin D. Roosevelt

We are not on this earth to fear anything.
We are here to love.
We are here to be loved.
In the end, it is the *best way* to achieve success and be rich.

How to Get Hired

Good luck in finding a job, my friend.

I know you will be a success in the beginning and in the end.

www.ingramcontent.com/pod-product-compliance
Lightning Source LLC
Chambersburg PA
CBHW031950190326
41519CB00007B/750

* 9 7 8 1 9 3 8 4 5 9 4 6 7 *